Habibo A Haji

Conquering *the* Odds

Journey of a Shepherd Girl

D1411745

Cover photo by Razaq Vance: www.razaqvance.com
http://photo.net/photodb
http://www.facebook.com/pages/Razaq-Vance
http://www.flickr.com/photos/31113121

ISBN: 0615768830
ISBN-13: 9780615768830

This book is dedicated to my children that they might read my story and know that the world is a very big place and not everyone lives like they do with so many comforts. I would like them to see that the world is full of many different cultures and where they live and how they live is a culture. It is my hope that they always believe in themselves and never ever give up. Life can be beautiful, but it can bring with it much sorrow and difficulty. However, difficulty and sorrow refine the soul making it even brighter than before.

I want all to know that this story is simply my story. There are many, many happy and beautiful stories from Somalia and Africa itself. My story is not indicative of all Somalia as mine is of village life. Life in Somalia cities is much different where people are more educated and civilized. In no way am I trying to say that all of Somalia or all Somali's lived as I did or suffered the things I suffered.

Contents

This, to Thine Own Self be True.

William Shakespeare

Introduction

———◆•◆•◆———

I was born in Africa the eastern coastal city of Mogadishu, Somalia. My father, wanting a son as his first born, was deeply disappointed when the hospital reported that I was a girl. So, shortly after my birth, he divorced my mother. Unable to take care of me by herself, my mother brought me to live with her mother, my grandmother, and her three sons in the small, primitive village of Balcad located in the southeastern region of Somalia. By primitive, I mean very primitive – no electricity, no cars, no phones, no motors of any kind, meals cooked outside over an open fire, herders and farmers living in small domed huts with dirt floors, crocodiles, jackals, hyenas, snakes and mosquitos carrying malaria. There, living with my grandmother, I suffered from physical and sexual abuse starting at the age of three.

By the time I was five, I was trained by my grand-mother to herd the sheep and goats out in the grasslands, where I had to chase off, not only hyenas and jackals, but boys herding their flocks as well who saw a young girl out by herself as easy prey. I was more successful at fending them off in the grasslands than at home in my grandmother's hut.

I survived the attacks of crocodiles at the river next to our village, as well as malaria, not once, but more than dozen times. By the time I was eleven, I was taking my grandmother's cattle deep into the grasslands, living as a nomad for months at a time with nothing to eat or drink except the milk I could get from the cows and the fruit and honey I could find in the wild. There, I learned what survival meant! I also learned how to depend on myself and myself only. I learned how to endure extreme hardship and loneliness, and I learned just how aggressive the young men herding camels could be, only wanting the thrills of rape to satisfy themselves when they saw a girl, the only girl, out by herself in the vast open grasslands. There I learned how to fight as well as hide without being seen!

I witnessed the breakout of civil war as Somalia fell to her knees into utter chaos, everyone fighting against everyone, tribe against tribe, clan against clan, everywhere! Because of the collapse of the country, thousands fled to nearby Kenya. I, with my mother and siblings, escaped to the largest refugee camp in the world – Dadaab in eastern Kenya, where I lived for three years.

There, I saw mothers and fathers each day carry the lifeless bodies of their children and loved ones, wrapped in an old blanket or cloth, to bury them outside the camp. There, I also witnessed women fighting each other with machetes or sticks or knives simply over their place in line to get water from one of four wells – four wells for one hundred and fifty thousand people! There, I witnessed the passive acceptance of seeing little children with very large stomachs and small skinny legs, dying, too weak to chase the flies away, their eyes pleading for help.

Memories! Memories which I thought were placed on a nice safe shelf in the back of my mind, often come flooding back to me where, I too, scratched out an existence within the hopelessness of Dadaab - the name itself sounding like something out of World War II: scenes of dysentery, cholera, unsanitary living conditions, people fighting over food and water, human waste everywhere, malaria being a household term, and no work or purpose or hope of anything better. I lived with the ever hungry beast called malnourishment, indiscriminately eating its fill of young and old alike.

I look back now, after spending the last dozen years in America learning English, becoming a U.S. citizen, going to school to learn the basics of reading, writing and math, and working toward my BS degree in nursing, working for one of the finest medical facilities in the world - the Mayo Clinic in Rochester, Minnesota.

I've tried to put my memories of fear and shame, disease, hunger...and rape out of my head, as now I'm thousands of miles away from Somalia. I've had the luxury of being so busy getting up on my feet in America, that I haven't had the time to think about where

I came from or what I'd been through. Perhaps I didn't want to think about it – until recently when I thought about writing my story.

Now, working as a Registered Nurse in a nice office with an eight-to-five job, my life in Africa and the struggles I've had to embrace there to survive, are fading into that area where memories can be carefully placed into perspective. That perspective helps me answer some questions like: Why me? What was the purpose of all this? How have I been so blessed to be where I am today?

My heart goes out to those around the world, of all nationalities, who are still struggling with extreme conditions of life and death, to those who can barely buy bread for themselves and their children, to those with little or no medical service to help with even the most common infections and disease, to those fleeing for their lives from the brutality and senselessness of war, to those victims of abuse and rape, and to those who have escaped but are living in a foreign land with no knowledge of the culture, the language, or how to succeed in life.

Being a first generation immigrant myself, from a country swallowed by chaos, I appreciate the tremendous effort that all immigrants had to make to leave their homeland and start from scratch to rebuild their lives.

My most recent memory of my home country is the life I led, along with one hundred and fifty thousand others, in Dadaab refugee camp. A camp which, established in 1992 to accommodate ninety thousand, has now swollen to one half of a million people and growing each day; growing not only by those fleeing for their lives across forests and deserts, being robbed and raped and murdered on the way, but by the ten thousand third-generation refugees born in Dadaab to their refugee parents, some of whom were also born there years ago. During the recent famine which struck Somalia, over one thousand people per day fled to Dadaab and set up camp. Some months saw as many as forty thousand seeking refuge! The famine has subsided, but the civil chaos has not. And the people remain!

Somehow, through great providence, I was able to leave Dadaab and Somalia, come to America, find work, educate myself and have my own family. My family and I are not living in a hut, or sleeping on the dirt, or looking for any handout of food we're given, but we own our home, buy our food from grocery stores like everyone else, send our children to schools, hire tutors, and live the American dream.

I'm hoping to share my story with you, not that it's so unique, but because it isn't unique. It's similar to the stories of many, many people: people who have struggled from one mouthful of food to the next, people who have endured extreme physical and mental hardship, and people who still aren't sure whether they'll see the sun go down tonight or the moon rise. People who pray, sometimes without hope, that they and their children might be spared from disease, murder, rape, and starvation.

Chapter One

Given to My Grandmother

———◆·◆·◆———

For fourteen years, my grandmother, Halima, was the only mother I ever knew. In fact, I called her Hoyo, which means "mother" in Somali. As a baby, I slept with her on her filiq, or mat woven from grass. And, each day, she'd carry me on her back using a long "morro," or piece of cloth, tied in the front as she walked the goats and sheep through the grasslands to graze. I had plenty of fresh air and sunshine as a baby, because I was walked through the grasslands each day, every day until I was about three years old and too heavy to carry. The milk Grandma fed me was very accessible, as she'd simply milk one of the goats or cows and feed me as she herded the animals. She told me when I was older that I was the easiest baby to take care of. I remember rubbing her feet for her a lot, when I got a little older as she was always out walking the animals.

My grandmother is still living in her hut in the small village of Balcad located approximately fifty miles south of Beledwayne on the eastern side of Somalia. She's a very intelligent woman who has gone through a tremendous amount of hardship in her life. She was married at the older age of sixteen through an arrangement made between her parents and her husband's parents. She became pregnant right away, and when she was four months along, her husband suddenly got ill and died, leaving her all alone and almost ready to give birth.

She moved back to her parent's village, Balcad, and gave birth to her son, my uncle, Abdi. When he was three years old, her parents arranged another marriage for her with a man named Qamac, who was quite a bit older than she was. They were married for five years and had two more boys, my uncles Ahmed and Abdi. Unfortunately, her luck with husbands wasn't very good, because when she was twenty four, Qamac died leaving her with the three boys to raise by herself. This was not a good situation for her, and in Somali society, especially back in those days, it was hard to find a husband once you were widowed, unless your late husband's immediate male relatives were willing to "Dumaal" you - offer you a hand in marriage, which happened quite often. The main reason for Dumaal was to protect the children from harm's way providing them with a home and parents. In my grandmother's situation, however, none of her late husbands had any brothers to marry her, so she lived by herself for several years before she met my grandfather, Ali.

After meeting my grandfather and getting married, she moved into his hut, and they worked together to raise the three boys. It didn't take very long for her to realize their marriage was destined to be troubled. My grandfather had a great heart, but was very quick with his temper and his fists. They often had verbal fights which almost always led to physical fights. In Somalia, there are no laws against domestic violence. In fact, there are very few laws against anything; people are just left to work it out themselves.

Shortly after their marriage, my grandmother got pregnant again with her first daughter, my mother Khadija. However, after giving birth, Grandma asked for a divorce, because my grandfather was just too volatile. My grandfather agreed on one condition – he was to keep Khadija. My grandmother reluctantly agreed and left my mother with him when she was only five months old. I can't imagine what that felt like for my grandmother; it must have broken her heart to give up her only daughter. Most women would say, "No way, there's no way I'd give up my daughter like that." But, remember where this occurred – Africa! There, the husband is king. Men rule. It would have been almost impossible for my grandma to go against her husband.

Initially, my grandfather took my mother to live and be cared for by his own mother, who lived in the same village in her own hut. Then he remarried again, taking his new wife, and my mother, with him to Jawher, a village about a hundred miles south of Balcad.

My grandfather earned his living as a religious teacher and would be gone every day, all day, teaching in the mosque, while his wife spent her days out in the grasslands herding and grazing the animals, carrying my mother on her back. Similar to how all babies are raised out in the villages, when she was old enough to somewhat care for herself and too heavy to be carried on her mother's back, she was left alone in the hut for the entire day until my grandfather and his wife got home.

In the villages, there are no toys, except for the ones the children can make themselves. Frankly, I think it develops creativity in a child. So, my mother would play with whatever small things she could find – sticks, rocks, even the dirt just like I and all the other toddlers did. What else would a three year old play with who is alone in a hut in Somalia? Out in the villages, there are no Walmarts, plus money is hard to come by so toys are just out of the question. My mother told me that sometimes a neighbor lady would bring her food, and after she ate the food, she'd take a nap on the bare ground outside the hut under a big tree. This is one thing in Somali villages that is very good; everyone looks out for everyone else's children like one big extended family. And, in a sense it is one big family since everyone is from the same tribe and clan with shared ancestry.

When my mother was old enough to do house chores, probably about five, she would work every day, cleaning, doing laundry in the river, cooking, and carrying water from the river for their cooking and cleaning needs – the normal life of a young village girl! One might ask, "What about education?" My friends, there is no education! The boys are taught some basic math, the Quran, and some reading basics.

Eventually, my grandfather and his second wife divorced, more than likely because of his temper. This time, he kept the two boys he and his wife had together along with my mother. So now, my mother, at eight years of age, became a mother to her stepbrothers and a surrogate wife taking care of the cleaning, cooking, laundry, etc. Sadly, if she messed up in any way, my grandfather would be unhappy, very unhappy and lose his temper. My mother, however, with no other place to go, stayed with him and raised her brothers until she was of marrying age herself - fifteen.

Her marriage with my father was an arranged one also, their parents being second cousins in an arranged marriage themselves. Without even meeting each other, they were married, my father being nineteen. Their fathers decided it would be good for them to be married, since it was more or less "in the family" or in the same tribe, and it would be easier than bringing in a whole new family with their relatives to deal with.

After they married, they moved to the big city of Mogadishu. My mother got pregnant with me shortly after their marriage. She tells me the story of when I was born. My father and his mother took her to the hospital in the afternoon where she was told that she couldn't leave until the next day. At that time, the hospitals did not provide food for the patients; family had to provide that. Unfortunately for my mother, no one brought her food. She was just left there all alone to give birth to her first child. She stayed all night in labor crying a lot, lonely and scared. In the morning before sunrise, she had her baby – me! My father, she told me, came in the morning and asked at the desk what the sex of the baby was. They said she had a girl, and he left. He didn't even go in to see my mother or bring her anything to eat or drink. Later that afternoon, he returned and took us home. Divorce came soon after. My mother, unable to support herself, went back to live with her father.

He was delighted to have my mother come back home, as she could help take care of his children, and her new baby as well. So, it seemed like a good arrangement. Except for the fact that my grandfather's temper continued to burn, and he continued with his violence towards those around him. My mother told me how difficult it was taking care of her siblings and a newborn baby. She had no time for herself, and the boys were difficult for her. Her roles of mother, sister and daughter were very difficult for her, so after some time, she decided she could no longer stay in that environment and planned to run away with me to my grandmother's village.

She quietly sold the few things she had to her name, so she could afford bus tickets for us, along with a little milk for me. One night, while my grandfather and the boys were all sleeping outside the hut which is the custom for males, she quietly got up while the hut was very dark, and gathered together our meager belongings and whatever clothes we had. Thankfully for her, we didn't have much. She wrapped me in a small blanket and tried very hard to keep me from crying. As quickly as she could, she snuck out into the dark of the night silently walking so as to not wake my grandfather who was sleeping on the ground as he always did. She told me that she was so afraid that he would wake up and find her leaving. Making it past my grandfather, she quietly walked out of the open gate in their fence made of branches and tree limbs and, without looking back, slipped away into the night.

She walked quickly through the dark paths of Jawher, while the whole village slept. Taking the trail through the countryside, she walked the four miles to where the bus stopped every morning. She told me that she was so relieved when we finally boarded the bus, always looking over her shoulder, fearing that her father would come at any moment to get us.

The bus ride to my grandmother's village, which I myself took several times later in my life, took about six hours taking the main roads. Getting off at a small little bus stop out in the middle of nowhere called Trejenta, she then had to walk the twenty six miles through the bush and along small donkey-cart paths to get us to Balcad.

The way was difficult for her, as there were many wild animals in the area, not to mention stray men that would lurk along the path waiting to rob or rape as people came by – and she had to carry me as well, along with our belongings. Later in life, I walked that same path by myself several times. Believe me, it was scary, and not at all difficult for a young girl or woman to get robbed and raped by roughians along the way.

The path wound around farmer's fields, through heavy bush, around ponds and marshes and through lonely areas. I know this was hard for her at only seventeen years old, but I think I inherited some of that strength and determination myself. I'm glad she had it in her.

My grandmother was not expecting us, as there was no way to communicate with her beforehand – no mail or phone service in the bush of Somalia! So we just arrived at her hut late in the evening. My grandmother was very happy to see her only daughter and new granddaughter, and welcomed us into her hut. She was so excited, that she told my mother she would slaughter a goat in the morning, and we'd have a feast according to tradition to welcome visitors, cooking it over the open fire and enjoying the feast with loved ones.

My mother enjoyed several weeks of peace with my grandmother, but it didn't take long for my grandfather to find out by word of mouth where she had gone. Word of mouth is the main form of communication out in the villages – slow, but it works. He was very upset that she left his house, making a mockery of his authority. Plus, he needed her to take care of his children and home. So, after a few weeks, he came after her, making the long bus trip and walk through the bush to Balcad.

He arrived at my grandmother's hut the night before Ramadan. My grandmother, according to tradition, was outside cooking the midnight meal. Many words were said that night outside her hut, both my mother and grandmother arguing with him to let my mother stay. His response was, "You need to leave with me right now. The boys need you and I need you to raise them. He demanded that my mother return with him to his village, or he threatened to beat her.

My mother refused to bring me back to his home and insisted that she be able to stay with me at my grandmother's hut. My grandfather, however, said, "You are my daughter, and you're coming with me."

She pleaded, "What will I do with my baby?" She looked at me and started crying.

His only answer to her was, "I don't care, you are my daughter, and you're coming with me!"

My mother agreed seeing how this was going to go. My grandmother, bless her soul, told my mother, "Don't worry, I will take care of her." She offered to keep me with her and raise me as her own child, knowing that it would not be good for me to be brought back to live with my grandfather where malaria and cholera were even more prominent than in grandma's village. She tells me, that she took one look at me for the last time, tears running through her cheeks. My mother reluctantly agreed, as she was not able to go against what her father said. I can't imagine how difficult this must have been for her to make that kind of decision. As a mother myself, I cannot fathom what I would do if I were placed in the same predicament.

My mother then returned with him to his village to take care of his children and household, leaving me behind to stay with my grandmother, where I remained until I was fourteen years old. I did not see her again until many years later. She would come and visit us from time to time, every few years, and each time she came, I longed to leave with her and stay with her, but I did not have the confidence or the courage to ask her. Looking back at it, though, my grandmother and uncles would have probably refused to let me go, as I was needed to help with the work.

I've wrestled with my feelings about being left with my grandmother. But looking back on the situation, really, what could my mother have done? She had no place to raise me, no husband to help her, and a father that was impossible to say no to. I'm very glad that I didn't have to live with my grandfather. And, life being what it is, my future was with my grandmother and three uncles in her village. I was to embark on the life of a shepherd, similar to many, many village girls and boys.

My mother and I have spoken many times about this turn of events in our lives. I understand it, and don't blame her. However, I still felt that I was abandoned, that my father didn't want me because I was a girl, and my mother left me because she didn't want to take me with her.

Chapter Two

The Village

———•◦•◦•———

Balcad became my home. The Ethiopian border runs about one hundred miles to the east, and the Indian Ocean three hundred miles to the west. The Shabeelle River, where everyone in the village got their water, washed their clothing, swam, watered the animals, and tended their gardens – the life blood of the area - runs north and south about one half mile from the village. In fact, every day, I'd go to the river to gather water for the day, give drink to the animals, and sometimes just to rest and swim.

Balcad, like many of the villages around it, has about thirty huts, each one surrounded by a fence made from poles and branches to keep the domestic animals in and the wild animals out. Approximately three hundred men, women, and children live there, along with all their cows, sheep, goats, donkeys and a few chickens here and there. Surrounding the village life thousands of miles of grasslands, scrub, bush, and forested areas where the people graze their animals.

My grandmother's hut, like all the rest of the huts in the village, is made of tree limbs tied together like an igloo and covered with grass woven mats, can house an average of about four people – mom, dad, and a couple of young children. If there are more children, especially older males, they sleep outside the hut on the ground, except when it rains, then everyone tries to crowd into the hut – sitting room only! The huts are built of long grass, woven into many "filiq," or rugs, which are used to cover a frame made from about twenty tree limbs tied together to form a rounded structure with a wide open door on one side which can be covered by a filiq in bad weather.

Each family has one hut, or maybe two or three, depending on how many of the children are married and living at home helping with the animals and crops. Each family encircles their huts with a tall fence made of tree branches and limbs to keep their animals in at night and the wild animals out; these fences are about two hundred feet in diameter with an open space at one end about six feet wide; we called this a "hero," or "contained area" as it contains the huts, and the various corrals for the sheep and goats and however many cows each family has.

The living space for each family is outside. The cooking area centers around a fire pit made with rocks in a circle to cook on and maybe some shelves put together to hold a few pots and pans, bowls, some cups and spoons – sorry, no silverware. This also serves as the space where the family spends their time when not out grazing the animals, simply sitting out around the fire or under a tree.

My grandmother had two huts, one for herself and one for her oldest son, Abdi, who married and had a wife. Her other sons, Ahmed and Ali, slept outside under a large tree unless it was raining, then they would come inside with my grandmother and I. But, they had to sleep sitting upright in the corner as there was no room for all of us to lay flat in the hut.

There are many of these villages in this area of the country, each one about five miles or so from each other, all scattered across the countryside for many miles around the Shebelle River, as this is rich farming country in Somalia. My grandmother's "hero" is located at the end of the village by the river - actually very close to it, so that if it rains a lot, the river overflows and cuts the whole village off from the outside world.

There is one lane in and out of the village and one path from the village to the river to take when getting water or going swimming. Another well worn path leads to the open grasslands, millions of acres of it, where the villagers would take their animals to graze and get water at the river. The grasslands are part of a vast open grassland owned by no one except the country of Somalia but governed by the local clans and tribes. On this land we would take our animals to feed on the tall grass wandering as many as ten miles out in one day and then coming back before nightfall; believe it or not, children start doing this at about the age of five. In the dry periods which would occur twice each year, we had to take our animals out many, many miles and stay out for several months until the rains returned to the village and we could once again graze the animals within a day's walking distance. The age to be able to take the animals out as a nomad for several months is about eleven and almost always only teenage boys. I however, was the exception.

On the north side of the village, about a twenty minute walk, lies all the farm land belonging to the various families where crops of corn and barley are grown on plots of land, several acres large, handed down from generation to generation. And west of the village, near the river, is where families grow special crops like mangos and guava, watermelon, beans, lemons, onions, peppers and other good food to eat grown in smaller gardens. This area is very plush and beautiful like a park.

Everyone in Balcad, of course, knows each other, as is the case in each of the villages. And, most are related in one way or another being of the same tribe and larger clan – herein lays the trouble. Next to my grandmother's hero lives my mother's uncle with one daughter about four years older than me and three sons in their teens. Next to them was another uncle and so on. All the villages are interrelated to each other with intermarriage going back many years. The people are like a big family with many subdivisions.

The villages around Balcad all belong to the Hawaadle tribe which governs a large, large area of Somalia. This large tribe had many subdivisions within it, each one layered on top of the other getting progressively smaller until you got to the individual village. My grandmother's tribe is the Abdulle tribe, and the village and several of those around it are of the smaller Samater tribe which was further subdivided into the O-baker tribe. Each one of these tribes from small all the way up to the larger Hawaadle tribe is governed by an "Ugaas," meaning in English, "respected head." If one of them dies, then one of their sons takes over – never a daughter! Thus, it is important in Somalia to have sons.

On the other side of the Shebelle River from our village lived another clan of a different tribe, and most of the time, they didn't mix with the villagers on our side of the river, because they are of a different ancestry. There wasn't fighting amongst the two clans until war broke out, but there was an unspoken dis-association and absolutely no intermarriage between them. If intermarriage occurs, both husband and wife are rejected and have to live elsewhere. So even though it's a small area and people know each other, there are still divisions between them, "This clan, we don't associate with them, and that clan we don't associate with them, and this other clan we do associate with them," and so on. This is why it is easy to under-stand how Somalia, right now, and since 1991, has been fighting amongst itself, each clan against each other all over the country, so that it is now nothing but chaos – hopefully that will change.

The Shebelle River is a major focal point with much activity as it's the only source of water for the villagers as well as their animals. It has two main sections: one is used for getting water for the day, bathing, doing laundry, swimming or just relaxing by the river; and one for watering all the animals. These two sections of the river have their own special names: Durdur meaning "flows with energy," named this because there are lots of rocks and falls in it with turbulent water. It is also where the river splits into three separate smaller rivers. The animals are taken here, because there are no cliffs, and they can walk up to it and drink.

This was my favorite place to swim and play, although at times when it rained, it was hard to swim in it because of the turbulence that could sweep you off your feet and down the river, drowning. The other danger in this area was the crocodiles which played a game of their own with you. When it was the dry season, that was the best time to swim, because the water would recede and wasn't very deep. Sometimes we would go past the first branch of the river and explore the second, which was unbelievably rich with natural fruits like a "hidden valley," where the village kids and I played hide and seek. During the dry season, the villagers swim across one branch of the Durdur to get to the land in between it and the next branch, so that they can gather grass and leaves for the animals to eat.

The other main section of the river is called "Qard-heer" meaning "cliff," because on one whole opposite side of it ran a very steep cliff. This area of the river is used for getting water for the village, doing laundry, bathing, or just sitting by the water. It is also the favorite spot to swim, and many times during the day, lots of the young people of the village would be there swimming.

The river, when it rains, rises way above its normal level getting very dark and very violent. In that case, when we got our water for the day, we'd fill our bucket with water then pour a little milk in it settling all the dirt to the bottom leaving clear water on the top to drink.

Beyond the village and to the east lie the mountains – magnificent to look at, as the sun rises above them. They are about a day's walk away, and sometimes we'd go that far with the animals to find green grass.

Thus is my little village of Balcad, where I grew up. I close my eyes and imagine the village every day when I have a quiet moment. I relive my life there and my most peaceful moments hearing the birds singing, climbing the trees and looking everywhere over the village to watch the people in their activities, getting leaves from the trees for the cows, swimming in the river, feeling the rush of, "Am I going to be eaten by a crocodile." I remember the feeling at the end of each day, contemplating how I made it through another day without being eaten by a crocodile or attacked by jackals or hyenas. I can still hear the sound the crocodiles make when they're swimming in the water; it's a swishing sound, and if you were in the water and heard that, you're in major trouble. There were lots of them in the area.

When it rained, it was the best time, as the trees would be green and blooming, the cows and other animals would have plenty to eat; it was a good time of life, the purest of pleasures. When I'd be out with the animals and sit with them after they'd eaten, they were so content. Life felt good, perfect. Many times I'd play with the monkeys and talk to them. They knew when I was being nice, then they'd be nice, but if I yelled or got angry, they'd mock me. When my job or life gets stressful for me, when my husband and I don't agree, when I'm worried about tests for college, or bills, I close my eyes, sit back and remember. All in all, it was a beautiful place, and I was blessed to partake in it.

Chapter Three

Early Days

———•••———

Growing up in a small village out in the bush of Somalia is probably nothing like you would ever imagine. If you've watched programs showing village life in Africa with huts built with sticks and branches, covered with rugs made of woven grass, naked babies and children running around, goats, sheep, cows with big horns, crocodiles in the river, then this would give you an idea of how I was raised.

When not out in the grasslands carried on my grandmother's back, I'd crawl around the hut until I could walk. Then my world got a little bigger, playing outside the hut in the dirt, sitting under the large tree inside our fence, never too far from my grandmother. Babies in the village don't wear diapers and most wear no clothes until they get older – maybe three or four. With no diapers, babies just do their potty anywhere it happens. In the hut, outside in the dirt, even when being carried on someone's back.

When I was about nine months old, Grandma taught me how to squat and go to the bathroom just like all the little kids are taught. She'd sit down on a stool and have me face her. She'd hold my hands, and I'd stand in front of her; she'd have me squat down in front of her and go potty. Eventually, I learned how to do it and to go potty only in acceptable places, like outside the hut near the animal pens.

Grandma had a large herd of sheep, goats, and cows, so our milk was always fresh. We had no refrigerator, of course, because there was no electricity in the village, or the entire area for that matter, so we had to drink the milk throughout the day or it would spoil. Babies in the village are not given solid food until about the age of two. Thus, malnourishment is usually an issue to be concerned about. It was common to see babies with big stomachs due to lack of nutrition. The sad thing is that the villagers aren't aware that babies need solid food by the time they're one. Their lack of education and understanding is not their fault, but there is a definite need for people to teach about nutrition, cleanliness, and healthy living.

There wasn't a whole lot of affection going back and forth in village life. The villagers are country farmers, living off the land, grazing their animals, working hard every day in a very rugged environment in order to survive. Even compliments or recognition was nowhere to be found. Parents expect their kids to be task oriented, and believe me, Grandma was very task oriented. She was kind, but not very warm for a little girl growing up there. She was a country woman, farmer, shepherd, very strong and tough. That's how it was, just part of the culture.

Like all toddlers in the village, I spent most of my time in the hut or outside of it within the confines of our fenced in "hero." I didn't have any siblings or friends to play with, so I'd play with the dirt, bury myself, make little huts of my own, make my own baby dolls and parents out of sticks and twine, pretending that someday I also would have a family of my own to care for. This is going to sound odd, but I even made breasts on the mother doll out of goat dung, then wrapped a piece of cloth around them. I'd make hair out of a certain tree branch that when chewed, the top becomes soft looking like hair. I'd have them wear a "maro" or wrap and, if married, they'd wear a covering on their head, if not then they could show off their hair. I'd use water out of the water jugs to make pretend food for meals and use rocks as goats and cows and little babies. I'd even make little fences to keep the animals in. When I tell my daughters about how I used to play and the toys I'd make, they laugh at me and say that it's silly and gross. It was a lot different than their Barbies and Tinker Bell dolls and store bought play houses.

My play spot was next to the hut in the dirt, which was somewhat sandy, much like playing in a sand box. There was a big tree close to the hut where my uncles would sleep, and I'd play underneath it, too. I'd play by myself because the neighbors didn't have any kids my age, and my uncles were too busy, or just not interested, in playing with me. I was always warned not to wander outside our fence, so I ended up spending a lot of time by myself from a very young age, which prepared me for the long hours of being all alone when I had to take the animals out to graze. I quickly learned how to enjoy my own company. To this day, I have a hard time being real social. I'm kind of a loner, but you know what, I like spending time with me!

I found many ways to occupy my day: I'd play with the animals inside their fences; spend time with the baby goats and sheep, they were so cute, and I loved playing with them. I'd try to milk them, but of course, they had no milk. I'd wander in with the cows to pet them, but some didn't like that, and they'd turn around and butt me; one time one even threw me up in the air. After that I stayed away from the cows. When inside the pen with them, if you were lucky, you could run fast enough to get away; otherwise, they'd come and step on you.

As I got a little older, perhaps about three, my grandma became worried that I'd wander out of our hero, which could be dangerous, especially if jackals and other animals were around. So, she began to drop me off at my aunt's, who lived a few huts away from ours.

My aunt had three older boys, ages eight, eleven and thirteen. One of them, the oldest, was very bad to me - and his brothers. Each day, we were left alone with him to watch after us, and he would start his "playtime" which involved doing things we really shouldn't have been doing. I remember knowing it wasn't right, but I had no way of saying no or running away from it. He would abuse us and take advantage of us, doing things in front of us or to us, making us see things that we were way too young to see.

This went on for quite some time, until my grandmother realized what was going on with my cousins, and that I was in a bad situation. So, she decided not to take me there anymore. With that kind of behavior being ignored and not discussed and with no laws against it, nothing was ever said to the boy's mother. Instead, Grandma simply took me out with her again each day to graze the goats and sheep.

This kind of thing happened a lot in the village. It was common for the young men, once hitting puberty to take advantage of the younger kids for sex. They would do it with anyone, or anything, they could. And nothing was done to prevent it or stop it. Parents don't do anything to intervene, it's just ignored like it doesn't happen. I remember there was a young man in the village, perhaps sixteen or so that was very active sexually with the younger ones. He was actually talked about, praised that he was so virile and how active he was sexually. He got a lot of recognition because of it.

Sad, but true, this is a period of my life when sexual abuse became almost a daily occurrence, as it was with most of the other children in the village. When I got a little older, about four, Grandma decided it was alright to leave me by myself in our hut, while she went out with the animals. She'd be gone all day long from very early in the morning until almost sundown at night. She'd leave me with some milk and porridge to eat for lunch and a warning to stay within our fence and not wander outside. However, she did not warn me about others coming into our hero.

From down the lane, a young man, about fifteen years old, each day would walk past our hero to go to what we call "Dugsi," where the young men go for religious teachings and read the Quran. He saw me many times when he walked by and knew I was home alone. When Dugsi was over, rather than going back to his own hut, he would come to ours. This is when the trouble would begin, as he would come by and be mean to me, tease me, and many times be very rough with me, hitting me with a stick, and finally at the height of it, abusing me sexually. This happened quite often. I hated it when my grandmother and uncles would leave in the morning, as I knew this young man would be stopping in.

He told me many times, that if I told my grandmother, he would beat me very hard and do much worse things to me, so I kept it to myself to this day. I learned at a very young age to tell myself that it would be over soon and just bear with it, as there was nothing I could do to stop him. He had control over me. One time, I remember, my legs were so marked up from him hitting me with a stick, that I had to keep my dress always down to my ankles so that my grandmother wouldn't see.

I was very afraid of the consequences if my grandmother found out what was going on. I was afraid that she would beat me with a stick, as she often threatened, even though it was in no way my fault being a mere child and taken advantage of. The young man knew that I had this fear, and he fueled it by saying how bad it would be if I told, and what more he would do to me if my grandmother found out. This is how domination and abuse happens, through fear.

His threats of my grandmother beating me with a stick were not unfounded, unfortunately. I saw her anger in action many times. One day, in particular, when my seven year old cousin, Fadija, was molested by a fourteen year old boy. My grandma walked in on them, as he was having sex with her. She grabbed Fadija who was naked, got a long thick stick and beat her until she bled from her hips, her shoulders, thighs, hamstrings, everywhere. I was in shock and crying, wanting her to stop. Fadija was screaming. She was a bloody mess.

My grandmother didn't say anything to the boy, didn't even tell his parents – nothing! He just got up and ran away. Can you see why the young girls and boys, even older girls, never ever tell if they've been abused. It is a shameful thing for them, blamed that it was their fault, that they were promiscuous, asking for it, playing with the wrong people. Rape and abuse simply had to be absorbed into your soul.

In the villages there are no laws against child abuse - physical, emotional, or sexual. Everyone just agrees that it doesn't happen and ignores it, minding their own business. When it happens, you tell no one. My grandmother and I, one day, came upon a woman being raped. Grandma told me, "Just turn the other way and keep walking." So, we did.

When someone does that to you, you begin to think it's normal; normal to play with older boys, getting into sexual acts. I felt trapped emotional, and that I couldn't tell anyone about the young man who stopped each day and came into the hut. I needed to cry and scream and tell on him, but I was afraid of what my consequences would be – from my grand-mother! As a threat, she took me out to the bush one day, and told me that she would leave me out in the dark in the bushes for the hyenas to eat me, if I ever did something like that. Sadly, I knew she would!

Looking back at it makes me mad at everyone – everyone! My grandma, my uncles, my mother, every-one! I feel that if I was left alone like that, vulnerable, just a small child, then I should have been with my mother. Where was she, and why? Didn't I mean that much to any of them. Didn't my mother know what would happen to me?

This type of abuse continued the whole time I lived in the village. As an older girl, when out on my own with the cattle, it would happen to me. I couldn't tell anyone, my uncles, my grandmother, no one. I wasn't going to risk being shamed or punished, so I had to deal with it on my own. Zip it and lock it behind mem-ory lane. My fear of my grandmother, kept me silent. There was no place to cry for help. The same situation existed for the other children, especially the females.

I received the brunt of Grandma's punishments quite often growing up. When I was eight, we had a very dry season. Everything was parched and dead, and we had to take all the animals far out to graze them. It was a several-day's walk, as there was no green grass to feed them in our area. We had a cousin about ten years old who came with us with his family's goats and sheep. He and I would take the whole herd, his and ours, out grazing each day from our makeshift camp, while my grandmother and uncle, Ahmed, took the cows. This was my first experience as a nomad, staying out in the grasslands for a few months until the rains returned.

One evening, my cousin and I brought the herd home, and my grandmother asked us to go find wood for the fire, so she could cook porridge for supper. We went out a ways from the camp, and you know how young kids are, we got side tracked looking at all the gorgeous birds and monkeys. What eight and ten year old wouldn't get side tracked by monkeys? Well, we lost track of the time. We finally realized we'd been gone too long, so we gathered up sticks and branches and ran back to the camp where my grandmother was waiting. She was so upset; I could see in her face that she was really angry. She grabbed her walking stick at the front of the hut with one hand and my arm with the other, scolding me, asking what I was doing with my cousin out in the woods and why it took so long to get back? I didn't know what to say; I just told her we were watching the monkeys. Needless to say, I had many bruises the day after, as anyone would if they were beaten with a stick. My cousin just stood and watched; what else could he do?

Another time, my cousin, Ayana, who was about twelve at the time, came over to our hut while I was home alone. She said to me that she wanted to eat some of my grandmother's sugar, which was very precious to us, as it was hard to come by. So hard to come by, that my grandma had to save money or sell goats to buy it in Beledwayne. Sometimes we'd go for months with no sugar, so it was a precious commodity.

My cousin told me that my grandmother would never know if we took some, and that I shouldn't tell her. It was kept in a burlap bag sitting in the corner of the hut, so we untied the bag and ate some, maybe about a cup full. My grandma came home that night after being out all day with the goats and sheep and, because she had the bag tied in a very particular way which no one could ever tie the way she did, she discovered that it had been opened. She was very upset about it. She asked, "Who's been in the sugar?" I denied it, being only four and very afraid of her. She said, "Do not lie to me!" I cried and said, "Ayana came over, and we had some."

Grandma found a strong stick outside and beat me with it. I screamed and cried, pleading with her to stop. Then she tied my hands together in front of me and then tied them to one of the poles at the top of the hut, so I was hanging from it with my feet dangling in the air. I cried and cried begging her to let me down, but she wouldn't. She let me hang there for quite some time, until all I was doing was whimpering. My arms ached so bad, I thought they were going to pull out of my shoulders, but finally she let me down. I loved my grandma, but she could be a very strong disciplinarian.

Growing up, all I ever tried to do was make her proud of me, and take notice that I did a good job trying to get even a pittance of recognition or praise. All I did was try to please, please, please her. I'd take the cows out further, wash and groom them more often, stay out all day grazing them never returning home no matter what, fought off jackals and hyenas for fear of losing a sheep or goat, and wake up early to make tea for her. But, I never heard, "You're good, hard-working, precious. Good job, Habibo." No appreciation.

She was exceptionally strong, tough. Many times she could've done more for my confidence and well-being. There was no concern as to how I dressed; I dressed worse than anyone. I was the only one with sandals made from tires and had only one or two dresses that I'd wear day after day. I began to feel like no one wanted me. So, let me ask you. If you were being molested, would you tell?

When I first came to America, I tried very hard to forget the past: the shame, feelings of worthlessness, and anger that came with it. I busied myself with surviving and making a life for myself here in this country of opportunity. And, I was successful doing that. However, several years after being here, when my daughter was five years old, the same as I was when molested, everything came crashing down upon me.

A male cousin was staying with us for a few nights. One of those nights, I woke from a nightmare. I dreamed that this cousin raped my daughter. I was yelling "I will kill him. He will not live if he did this to my daughter. I was sweating, my night gown, sheets, and pillow were soaked with my sweat. I couldn't breathe crying as hard as I could.

That is when the PTSD started for me. After that night, I had nightmare after nightmare; I would have vivid images of what had been done to me. I'd fight in my dream and wake up gasping for air. Pretty soon, this reliving of my past consumed my life; I did not know what to do. I didn't have anyone to talk to and didn't have the resources to help me work through the issue. I tried to go on with life as usual, but my emotions and the pain was eating me alive.

Now that I'm older, away from the village, and had help sorting through my feelings, I can forgive them. Grandma, with no education whatsoever, did the best she could with what she had. Anger and hurt used to be my fuel. Pushing me to do better than anyone and show people, especially those that left me in that situation, and those that were there but did nothing to stop it. What fuels me now, though, is my kids and providing a good life for them. I want to show them through my own children, what it is to grow up loved and cared for, proud of yourself, and confident that you have someone to confide in without fear of repercussion.

Somali culture, as you can see, is very different than the western world. In the country, life concentrates on staying alive and survival, which means taking care of your animals, growing crops, and trying to get to the end of the day without getting killed in one way or another. Males are greatly valued; it is an honor to have sons, and they are pretty much allowed to do as they please, kind of like the sacred cows in India. Their aggression is simply worked around. Not all males are bad, though. My uncle, Ahmed, was, and is, a wonderful man. He tried to take care of me and watch out for me, but he also went about his own business, while I was either left alone at home, or out in the grasslands with the animals, where I always had to be on guard and prepared for the constant threat of rape and abuse.

I want to be a part of something to help change society, more than just me and my kids. If I can give back I will. The man upstairs has a plan for me, and shows me through my faith that something or someone is guiding me to make the right decisions - I can sense it in quieter moments. I feel OK now, heading where I need to be.

When I look at my three year old son who is learning and exploring the world around him, my heart melts with happiness and gratitude. I'm able to be fully present in his life, and able to teach him and help him get ready for school. He already knows his alphabet, numbers, shapes, and colors. He knows so much more than I did when I was eight years old. I'm thankful he does not have to grow up the way I did. More importantly, he doesn't have to wonder whether he's loved or not; I tell him every chance I get and show him with all my actions.

Chapter Four

Trained as a Shepherd

My grandmother had seventy five sheep, forty five goats and forty cows. Before I turned five, and as soon as I was able to keep up walking, she started taking me out with her to learn how to herd the sheep and goats. My uncle Ahmed was in charge of taking the cows out while my other uncle, Abdi, stayed at the farm with his wife to watch after the young calves, sheep and goats. Abdi had a lot of physical ailments, untreated tuberculosis for one, so he didn't go out so much but stayed back tending the young animals and taking care of the home site. My youngest uncle Ali was going to full-time Dugsi at that time. He left for Mogadishu when I was about 7 years old. I didn't see him until many years later.

Grandma Halima taught me all the paths to take through the grasslands as well as the daily routine of leaving the village the same way for two miles, navigating through the crop land and keeping the animals out of the farmers' fields, then finally out to the big open grasslands and wooded areas. She had her stick to carry with her, and, of course, I had to have mine. She was very patient, teaching me all the various whistles and sounds to use to direct and call the herd. She also carried a little bell with her, which she'd ring, and when she did, all the sheep and goats would come running together. She'd mainly use it if we were in a wooded area to keep the herd together, or if she needed their attention, she'd ring it like she did when taking them to the river or bringing them home at night.

Around midday, when the sun was highest in the sky - we'd take the herd back to the river to drink and rest. These were the times I fondly remember, as we'd sit by the river watching the animals; sometimes we'd talk, sometimes not. Many times I would lie in her lap and fall asleep. And, after about an hour or so, we'd head out to the grasslands again until the end of the day walking, walking and walking some more, then finally, we'd start heading home for the night.

She wasn't always very talkative when we'd stop and rest; I was more afraid of her, or maybe respectful is a better word. I was just concerned about her and not very comfortable with her; perhaps she had to be tough living on her own as she did. I was more on edge and worried about my performance and getting punished if I did poorly. I loved her very much, but she never hesitated to give me a correction or sometimes a swat on the bottom with a stick. Don't get me wrong, I have good memories laying on her shoulder and cuddling when going to bed, but when we went out in the grasslands with the animals, I had to be more focused, because the sheep and goats were our livelihood - without them, we'd starve. So, unfortunately, even at the early age of four or five, I had a hard time relaxing; I felt anxious a lot and more tense than most young girls that age.

One of the first or second times we went out into the grasslands, we had two sheep ready to give birth. Grandma helped one have its baby, and I got to watch. She explained everything to me, showing me how to help the baby come out, making sure it was turned the right way, and comforting the mother. After it was born, she said, "OK, Habibo, the next one you can help, since you're going to be taking care of them, and you'll need to know how to do it." So, the first thing I did when the sheep's water broke, was rub the liquid around the sheep's bottom to relax it, so that it could be more flexible and stretch for the baby lamb to come out. Usually, the feet come first, so I took hold of them – they were all wet and hard to hold onto, then I had to gently rotate the lamb out and pretty soon, "Bulla" - there's the lamb!

One of the worst times I had helping a sheep give birth was when I was a few years older, around six, and out herding on my own. One of the goats was going to give birth, and, of course, it was way out in the grasslands, several miles from the village. Well, one foot came out but not the other. The goat was struggling really bad and couldn't walk anymore, so I had to stay there with her. The two girls that I was with that day said, "Just leave it, who cares?" But I said, "No, I'll be in big trouble and get whipped if I lose a goat."

I was even more worried that the poor mother would be eaten alive by hyenas during dark time when they came out to hunt. So, the girls left me out there in the grasslands all by myself, while they took their herd and mine back home. I was crying and crying, not knowing what to do and certain to get into trouble if I lost a sheep. I got on my knees and prayed to God that somehow I'd be saved from this situation. It was getting dark, and I was so afraid being out there all by myself. Finally, this man came by walking towards the village; he was older and very nice. He offered to carry the goat back to the village. I was so grateful for his help; the goat lived, and the baby was born with the help of my grandma.

One of the last times before I went out on my own with the herd, my uncle, Abdi, took me out, further than my grandma ever went, and showed me the way to take the animals through the grasslands as far as Mount Burdeer, saying, "Habibo, this is as far as you can go." The day was cut short because it was Ramadan, and he had to fast, meaning no food or water. Being foolish, I forgot to bring my water with me, and there was none in sight, as it was the dry season. We walked and walked for what seemed like forever until about midday, when the sun was right above our heads. By that time I was very thirsty and said, "Uncle, I'm thirsty." He answered, "I'm sorry, there's no water." No one lived around there for us to stop and get water as we were in a very vast open land with no people. Abdi said, "OK, you can go back, I'll keep going."

So, I started walking back home. I remember the sun shining directly into my face, and it was very hot, 115 degrees or more. I was wearing sandals made out of old tires, and when it's hot out, they get super hot. The tire shoes were the cheapest of all shoes, and most all of the girls didn't wear them. But, being me and not having someone to say, "No, she is a girl and needs better shoes," that's what I wore.

Walking back through the dry, dusty grasslands, I kept seeing mirages of water in the distance, and I'd think, "OOOhhhh water!" But I'd walk and walk, eventually getting out of the bush area and into dry empty land and the mirages just became one vision after another. It was stark with no vegetation, and the ground was hard as a rock. I walked a long way, for several miles. Being the dry season, there wasn't even one of the trees that when it's dry out, it has fruit you can eat and get some moisture. I kept walking, thinking, "I'm getting close! I'm getting close!" Yet, no water!

I finally couldn't walk anymore, because my feet were burning tremendously. I took my shoes off as I was getting blisters all over my feet, and finally walked barefoot. The last thing I remember was feeling very light headed, barely able to walk another step. I really needed to sit down, but couldn't. I knew that, if I wanted to live, I needed to get to either a water hole or home which was still at least ten miles away.

I must have passed out, because the next thing I remember is waking up in a nomad's shelter which was little more than some branches put together with a woven rug thrown over it to keep the sun out. When

I gained consciousness, I was alone with just the man there with me, because his wife was still out with their herd. He told me he came from a trip to the city and was walking home, when he found me laying on the ground in the bright sunlight. I recognized him from when I was out with the animals with my grandma, and our paths would cross, so I wasn't scared. Plus, he was of the same tribe as my uncles. I asked him, "How did I get here?" He said, "I picked you up, because you were passed out in the desert with no one, all by yourself. When I got you home, I gave you cold water, and you took a few sips, and I patted you with water to cool you off and waited until you woke up, because I don't know where your hut is."

I remember telling him that I was so thirsty, so he gave me a big water jug. I finished it so fast, that I started vomiting up water. His wife came home late in the day and gave me some milk to drink, "Slowly," she said. By this time it was dark out. She asked me where I lived, and I told her.

The man took me home, and we got there about 9:00 or 10:00 at night, very dark out, to find my grandma and uncles sitting around the fire having dinner. They didn't know where I was, and they were worried, yet not so worried that they came out to look for me. Instead, they scolded me. They said, "Why would you do that, Habibo, leaving your water jug at home?" They drilled me with questions as to why I didn't bring my water with me, and how could I be so stupid. The man said, "This child was passed out in the desert. She was so thirsty. How could you leave a child out like that?" Abdi was there eating his dinner and said, "Well, she didn't take water with her; she should've taken water."

That was a tough lesson for a five year old girl. But you can be sure I never forgot to bring water on a trek like that again. I realize, of course, my uncle Abdi should have made sure we had water along, but young children are expected to grow up very fast when they live out in the country in order to survive. They also have to be independent enough to herd the animals at that young age.

Shortly after this, my grandma and uncles decided I was ready to take the sheep and goats out by myself, but first they wanted me to spend some time taking the herd out with our two neighbor girls, Sarah and Alma. They were about ten or eleven years old and had been herding their animals together since they were five. I was excited to now be able to be on my own with no one watching my every move and always quick to correct me. And, I thought that I could now play a little more while the herd was grazing – maybe play with the other girls in the dirt and make my own dolls out of sticks.

I remember the first day we went out; I got up quite early, probably around 4:30 and was very nervous - all excited that I was going to go with these two older girls. I was excited to be going along like we could be friends, but what I didn't know was that they were going to be mean to me. After my morning chores were done, and the sun started coming up, my grandma made porridge for me for breakfast. I filled my tin bottle with water (something left over from when the Italians were in the country) and put the cork in the top - kind of like in a wine bottle. Grandma and I let the goats and sheep out of their pen and counted each one, so that when we saw the girls coming down the lane, I'd be ready.

Soon, I could see them coming down the lane that passed in front of our hero. We let our herd out, and they all mixed together just like that. Together with ours, we had about two hundred. It was an exciting start to the day, and off we went on our way out of the village into the wide open grasslands. The herd started moving and pretty quick, off they went. We took them through little paths that wound their way through farmers' crop lands having to make sure they didn't get into their fields. One of the girls was in back of the herd, one on the side and I was on the opposite side, while the fastest goat was leading the whole pack. Once we got past the crop land, we just let them go.

We didn't bring any food with us, only water. If you were lucky, you could find some fruit out in the land, but we had nothing else to eat. I quickly learned that the two girls were not going to be friends with me. Instead, they ended up being bullies.

As we were out in the grasslands, we'd run into other young people with their herds out as well. The girls would get together with their own best friends talking and laughing, and I ended up being their gopher, as they'd have me do all the work, while they sat with their friends, saying, "Habibo, go get that sheep, Habibo run and get this, run and get that."

They and their friends would pick on me also, telling me that my clothes were not nice, or that I was not pretty, and they would make me do all the work for them and their friends. "Run here and do that, go over there and get that sheep, hurry up, go get those goats over there, Habibo." All the while that I was made to do these things, the older girls would be playing with other girls and teenage boys.

Sara, Alma and I did this every day for a few months, before I could be on my own. It was the longest few months of my life. Each day, by midday, we'd take the herd to the river. It was usually alright, except the girls would start swimming, and I didn't know how to swim, so they'd make me watch the goats and sheep. So, I did my best to talk to the herd to get them to them sit and rest for a while under the big trees by the river. After being there for an hour or so, we'd again take the herd out into the grasslands before bringing them home at night.

One time, after I wizened up, the girls wanted me to do their job and watch their herd for them, while they went off and played. I said, "OK, I'll do that," and just sat under a tree and ignored the herd. Most of the animals, especially those with babies, who were always wanting to get back to the village, left and went home. The girls were swimming and playing with the boys, having no idea that more than half the herd was heading back to the village. The girls came up to where I was sitting and said, "OK, it's time to count now."

They found that they were missing a few dozen, and I was missing about fifteen. They were very upset, saying, "Where did they go, where are they?" I acted stupid and said, "I don't know what happened." They were all in a panic and told me to stay with the herd, while they went to look around and search for the others, but they couldn't find any of them. Their plan then was just, "OK, let's finish up and go home later. We'll tell our parents we don't know what happened."

So, we went home by 3:00 in the afternoon, which is a big no no, being way too early to stop grazing. I remember them being so worried that they were going to get into trouble. I got home and my grandma asked, "What happened?" as here she was at home and all her sheep and goats came walking in through the main gate. I said, "We were swimming, and they escaped." For some reason, maybe someone was smiling on me that day, there was no punishment.

I continued with the girls for a few months, then came to my senses and realized they were just mean and cruel, so I preferred to go on my own and not mess with them and their herd. I learned to count at this age, because each day before I left home, and each night before I came back, I had to take an inventory of the livestock. The other children in the village had to do the same thing and, miraculously, all the animals knew which herd to stay with, and which compound was theirs to go home to at night. They would follow the lead goat and the shepherd – me - with my shepherd's stick. From that day on, until I left the village, I took the animals out every day, seven days per week, all year long.

Grandma taught me how to survive out in the wild, like how to save my supply of water so that it lasted through the whole day, or how to make ropes out of a certain tree bark that was real stringy. She was a good teacher. She taught me how to keep an eye out for other animals that would lurk around and try to steal one of the herd. I learned to listen for them. I'd hear them out in the bush, but not see them – like hyenas and jackals, bush pigs and the African wild dog. Jackals, mainly, would be around during the day, hyenas liked to come out at night.

The jackals would come around a lot in groups of maybe six or seven. They'd make a yipping sound, but were hard to see, as they look like the grass being grayish brown. So they'd find a way to sneak up on the herd and hide behind trees; then all of a sudden, when you least expect it, they'd rush out at the animals. The sheep would run like crazy in all different directions; they're the worst to take care of, as they have no sense of direction whatsoever. The jackals would chase them all over; I would run as fast as I could and yell at them shaking my walking stick, chasing them far enough away to make sure they didn't get any of my animals.

One time, however, when I was about six years old and out on my own, I wasn't able to chase them away. They have this trick of knowing where to bite to bring the sheep down, and they killed a baby goat and strangled a sheep. I was sitting far enough away and playing with other kids from a different village, when I noticed my goats and sheep were running off in opposite directions from me with several jackals running after them.

There was a baby goat only a few months old, and I could see the jackals were going for it. I jumped up and ran as fast as I could, but the jackal grabbed it, and the poor little goat was twirling in the jackal's mouth. I was running, running, yelling and chasing it as it was running with the goat in its mouth. I was screaming and yelling, trying to make as much noise as possible. The jackal did let go, dropped the baby goat and ran away, but I was too late. The little goat lay there in the grass, bleeding and having a hard time breathing. So, I sat by it and pet it, trying to soothe it and calm it down.

But then I had to chase after the other goats, because they were still running crazy. Once they calmed down and quit running, I came back to the one on the ground, but she was dead. There was nothing left for me to do, so I just walked away. I felt sick to my stomach, vomiting, shaking and afraid that I would get whipped for losing a goat - which I did that night! "Habibo, how could you not have your eyes open? How could you let that happen?" Believe me, that's hard to take when you're only six years old.

It must have been one of those days when you should not leave the house, as that same day, while watching the herd, I noticed the sheep were scattering, so I ran toward them, trying to see what the problem was. A large jackal got hold of a baby sheep and grabbed it on the side. There were two jackals after that sheep, so I threw my walking stick and hit one on the back, and it ran off. The other one was still running after another sheep, but once it noticed that its companion ran off, she did, too.

There's a saying in Somalia that hyenas and jackals understand, "If I knew which sheep belonged to a woman, I wouldn't touch it," meaning a woman's possessions are not to be touched. If you do, you're doomed, because she'll never forget it and mention it for the rest of your life. I think perhaps that's true in many situations with women, not just when it comes to sheep and goats!

I learned a lot about herding animals as well as life from Grandma. By the time I was ten or eleven, I was taking the herd of cows out rather than the goats and sheep which Grandma took over. One of the most important things she taught me, was how to be patient with the animals - especially the cows. They'd fight, or all go in different directions, so it was easy to get frustrated and upset. But, with cows you can't do that. You have to find a way to take care of the situation without making it worse. You have to talk to them, tell them where you're going like, "Go to the river, go home, let's go this way, let's go that way." And, I also learned to sing to them in many different ways to soothe them and keep them calm. Each one of the cows had names, so I could call them by name like Dinjar, which means bright red - and he was bright red.

When they were full from grazing, they'd all lie down and get comfortable. This was a nice time for me, as the walking would end for awhile, and I could sit down with them, especially my favorite cow, Dinjar. I would lay on her and pat her and talk to her, many times falling asleep with her. Some would seek me out when we'd be out in the grasslands and come and want to be petted also. Or, if they got a bug, I'd take it off - they were my friends, and I trusted them more than the kids in the village.

One thing about animals, they cannot disappoint you. What's not to like or love about them? The cows made me feel like I was responsible, as I'd take them far away if it was dry, graze them, find water, and feel a sense of accomplishment knowing I helped them make it through one more day. When I'd bring them home, the people in the village would say, "Oh, Habibo, your cows are full, they look so good." But really, it was my grandma I was hoping would give me a compliment or approval, but she didn't.

In the grassland were many shepherds, but you may not see them, because it was so big. Sometimes, however, there were some that would be close by. One day, I was by myself with the herd, and this lady came by from another village. It was about 4:00 in the afternoon; it rained some, but it cleared up and the rain went away. I was having fun with my animals, when the lady came and said, "Hi, how are you doing?"

I answered politely, "Good, how are you?"

She said, "What are you doing here? Don't' you know the Juhan is here, and he could eat you?"

As kids, we all knew about Juhan. The story in the village was that he was a wild beast type of man who would attack people, especially little children, so we all feared him. I freaked out when she told me this; then she started making hideous faces. I thought, "Oh no, she turned into Juhan, and she's going to eat me."

She said, "I'm going to get you little one," and started to chase me. I ran for a good thirty minutes non-stop, until I got all the way back home to the village. I just left the animals! Grandma said, "What happened?"

I was all out of breath and scared and just blurted out, "Oh, the Juhan lady was going to eat me."

Grandma laughed and said, "What are you talking about?"

I could barely speak. I was so afraid, and said, "She was going to eat me, I had to run."

"You're silly," she said. "There's no such thing as Juhan – just go back; there's no such thing." Ahmed, my favorite uncle, bless him, just laughed and laughed and walked me back to where the herd was still grazing.

One time, a younger girl from the village came along with me, so she could also learn how to be a shepherd. I was about seven and she was about five, and we'd graze our herds together. We took the herd back to the river to this really nice spot, where we could let the animals eat and play and lay by the river to rest. She and I had fun making little dolls out of sticks, with grass for hair and dressing them in leaves.

However, towards the end of the day, when it was time to get going, we started counting the herd. I realized we were missing one, even after counting many times over - and it was one of mine that we were missing. I started to panic. She counted hers, and they were all there. I started running around calling the goat's name and just couldn't find it. So, we went home knowing

I was going to get punished. I told my grandma that the goat was missing, and that it was the one that was missing one horn. I told her I didn't know what happened, and that I was watching all day. Surprisingly, Grandma was OK with it and didn't punish me.

She just said, "Let's hope she doesn't get eaten by crocodiles. Did you count them before you took them to the river?"

I told her, "I'm pretty sure she was there when I took them to the river. Whatever happened occurred after we got there."

She told me, "You're supposed to be more alert, listening for distress rather than playing."

So Grandma, Ahmed and I went back to the river and trailed all the way through the woods a long way, until it became open land. Calling and calling the goat's name and whistling for her, we heard a noise down near the river. We looked around, and made our way over to the cliffs that line one whole side of the river. Sure enough, we saw the goat. She had fallen down the cliff and was hanging by a little snag, almost ready to fall into the river. And to make it worse, it was an area known for its crocodiles.

My uncle was so mad; it was the only time I ever saw him upset. I have never seen him this upset before or since.

"What is this now?" he cried, "How do I get that sheep out now? I have to go into the river to get it out. I don't know what to do."

We tried to make some kind of a rope, but not in time - the goat ended up falling into the river. My hands were shaking, I was crying and afraid I'd pee myself. I was worried Ahmed would be eaten by a crocodile. Poor Ahmed; it was such a wide river and very dangerous.

The water was turbulent, and the goat went with the waves down the river. Ahmed and I ran and ran by the bank of the river, watching her the whole time. But my grandma couldn't keep up. The goat tried to swim but kept being pushed farther and farther into the river. Grandma just couldn't keep up, so Ahmed and I kept running. All of a sudden, Ahmed jumped into the river ahead of the goat and grabbed her by the horns. Poor Ahmed, he had to swim to get her out, as the water was deep and running pretty fast. This time I did get a scolding. Ahmed and Grandma were mad at me and told me to never do that again. Luckily though, I didn't get whipped – how on earth did I pull that off?

Ahmed got over being upset. Since he was a noble man, one day when I was seven years old, he said to me that if his beloved sheep named Dhexyar gave birth to a female sheep, he would give it me. I was beyond excited. I was so happy, as I have never owned anything in my life before that moment. I was determined to take care of my sheep now, and I was so glad that I could have something of my own. I decided that I was going to name her Fahmo, because that was a name I always liked.

His sheep did indeed give birth to a female lamb. I named her Fahmo and tended her every chance I got. She started walking right away, and I got super excited. I went to bed at night feeling fabulous thinking that my life had a new meaning now. Two nights later we had a big storm. It started raining after I went to bed, and for a child who has been on her feet for longer than twelve hours, I did not wake up during the storm.

My grandmother woke me early in the morning as usual, and the first thing I did was check on my little Fahmo out in the pen set aside for baby sheep and their mothers. There she was, sleeping peacefully on the side of the mother sheep. I tried to wake her up, but couldn't. I figured something was terribly wrong and, getting very upset, I called my grandmother out. She came, wondering why I was so hysterical, so I told her that something was wrong with my little Fahmo.

Grandmother took one look and felt Fahmo's neck saying, "Sorry, hoyo, your sheep has died."

I was so devastated that my sheep died; I thought that I was "bacaaw" meaning the bad luck one. Because some of my family members used to say that I was bacaaw; so I thought to myself that this confirmed my unluckiness. I felt so bad, but, like many children that live on farms and learn the lesson of having an animal die, I had to get over that. I knew that life moved on, and there were many others in the herd to take care of.

Crocodiles! One other time, when I took our goats and sheep to the river to drink, I was sitting back on the bank just watching them and talking with my neighbor. It was about midday, extremely hot, and the animals were very thirsty. They all lined up in a row at the edge of the river with their mouths down to the water. We were talking and visiting up on a grassy hill, and as we were watching them, all of a sudden they all stopped drinking and lifted their heads - all in unison at the very same time! It was very odd to see, almost like it was choreographed. Then the whole herd, at the same time, started to walk backwards looking straight ahead at the water, thinking to themselves, "What is wrong with this thing?"

All of a sudden, we could see one of the younger sheep bent over with its butt sticking out of the water. We stood up quickly, just in time to see a crocodile with the young sheep's head in its mouth. It quickly twirled around in the water with the sheep in its mouth and dove beneath the surface - sheep and all! You know, when those crocodiles peer above the water and pick you out as their meal, you're picked out! It does it's best to get you; it just hones in on its prey.

When I was ten, going on eleven, Grandma told me, "I think you're old enough to take the cows out like the rest of the children your age." So, I started taking the cows out, and my grandma took over with the care of the goats and sheep. With cows you have to be fast to keep up with them. And, you have to be willing to go far, as they like to walk and walk and walk. They can eat much more than goats and sheep, so they travel far to get a full stomach of grass. When I'd take them out, I'd let them just start walking and follow each other, as they'd follow the fastest walker.

I'd also have to be able to break up their fights. We had three bulls, and the rest were cows for a total of about fifty at any given time. The most difficult part of herding them was when the bulls would fight. All you could really do was go as far away as possible from them, or they'd kill you, charging at you if they were mad. I was afraid of them. Usually, if they were fighting, I would ignore them, but I had many close calls. The whole village had about ten bulls, and they knew each other and wouldn't stop until one of them would win. We had the cutest one, gorgeous, so everyone wanted him to breed their cows.

The biggest mistake I ever made was trying to break them up one time when our favorite one was involved. Another herd from the village was grazing fairly close to my herd, and their bull, a very large one, started fighting with ours. I felt sorry for him, getting beat up by this huge bull. My bull fell down, and the other was butting it with its horns. So I took my walking stick and hit the large bull on its side as hard as I could trying to scare it off, but he in turn charged after me. He turned around and snorted at me and pawed the ground, then charged with his head down and horns pointed directly at me. I was lucky though. I ran like crazy, got behind a tree and grabbed onto it; he looked at me really angry like, "I want to kill you real bad," but I guess the tree was more imposing, and he went back. In the meantime, my young bull ran away. So, I guess I broke up the fight, but I could've been the one that lost the fight rather than my bull.

One time I was herding the cows by myself, when some bad boys - two boys in their older teens, wanted a farmer's crop, so they let their cows eat his barley. After their herd stripped his field, they took their cows and left. I didn't know this was happening between them and the farmer. As I was walking my cows home, I saw the farmer, just furious, walking towards me. I knew him and thought, "He's one of the Tumalles." Well, he came towards me with a long stick. He said, "How dare you let your cows eat my barley."

"I don't know what you're talking about. I didn't do anything. My cows didn't do it."

He hit me twice with his stick, and I started to run as he ran after me. I fell, and he grabbed me and whipped me again. I ran and ran, but he couldn't catch me. Then he took my whole herd of cows to his home. I ran home crying and bleeding, and my uncle, Ahmed, said, "What's going on, what's happening."

So I told him about the farmer. He said, "He hit you?" He was furious. So he went after the farmer, but by that time the man cooled down. He told Ahmed, "I'm sorry. I found out it wasn't your cows; I shouldn't have done that, I was angry. Someone else told me it was not your cows." So Ahmed scolded him, "How dare you whip my niece like that, her being such a young girl." The farmer said to Ahmed, "I will give you a goat for that," but Ahmed let him off.

I had many experiences in Africa which would seem very strange or scary to people living in the western world, but to us, it was just part of daily living. Many incidents occurred down by the river, as it was a focal point for the village as well as for wild animals.

One time, when we were swimming in the river, I saw a hippopotamus. My uncle, Ahmed, told me to be very careful, that if you got close to it, it would cut you in half. I remember that it lived in the river near the village, and every now and then it would pop up out of the water and blow all its water into the air. After a few years, however, it was no longer there. Perhaps the crocodiles got it, or maybe it just moved on to another spot.

The crocodiles were nothing to mess with, as you can imagine. Once in a while, they'd come up to the shore and eat a goat or baby calf that was drinking by the side of the river. Sometimes they would actually kill people. When one was spotted, everyone would call the young men in the village, and they'd try to get it and kill it before it caught and killed someone. Many times I saw them trying to catch a crocodile, splashing in the water, trying to throw a rope around it. It was a pretty active sight.

I actually did see one that ate a young girl; it was humongous! We were all down by the river swimming and enjoying the coolness of the water, when all of a sudden there was a big splashing. We all looked over at the sound to see this huge crocodile grab one of the younger girls by her head. She was flailing with her hands and kicking, but it twisted around really fast, its tail powering it around, and it pulled her into the water. It all happened so fast. We all started screaming and trying to help her, swimming towards her, trying to grab her legs as she was kicking, but it was too late. The crocodile dove under the water with the girl in its mouth, and that was the last we ever saw of her.

Later that day, the young men were able to capture it; they killed it and brought it out of the water and cut it in half, but the girl wasn't in it. She probably was left under the bank of the river or in some weedy area, as crocodiles take their prey and hide it in the river, then eat it later. Usually we knew where to swim and not swim to avoid the crocodiles. If the river had waves on it, it was safe, but if the water was still in certain areas then you're in trouble.

Monkeys also lived near the river as lots of vegetation grew there. They were very mischievous and would throw nuts and pods of seeds at us, when we were by the water. They would then put a finger in their mouth and make a sound like when we stick out our tongue and blow out; then they'd laugh and screech if they were successful in their throw. They also would imitate us. If we had to go behind one of the trees to relieve ourselves, they also would go behind a tree and squat down, then put their hand to their mouth and laugh.

Village life kept everyone busy with work, young and old alike, so I didn't have much time to play with kids and socialize. We didn't have any school, as what else would we need to know except herding the animals, planting crops, having babies, and building huts? I couldn't write or read, but I was no different than any of the other young people, as neither could they. I resented the work at the time, of course, but now I see that I was able to learn to be a very good worker, take direction from others, and learn patience to bear with difficulty until it passes – very good qualities for my job as an RN at the Mayo Clinic.

Chapter Five

A Day in the Village

————◆◆◆————

My immediate thought, when I think of going back to the village, has always been, "Absolutely not, no, never, never again." However, quite a few years have passed since I've been in Balcad, and I'm finding that I really don't remember the bad so much, or maybe it's that I am forgiving life for the bad it held for me. I'm remembering the good – and there was good in village life, as nothing in this world, I believe, is one hundred percent evil. I learned that good permeates all, even if it's in small portions. Actually, I'd enjoy going back to Balcad, just not permanently. Sometimes I close my eyes and imagine I'm there sitting by the fire and cows, hearing nothing but the sounds of hyenas, birds, and of course my animals.

I remember the environment that it was set in; it was so beautiful, verdant and lush in the rainy seasons, hot and dusty in the dry season. Twice each year, we were blessed with plentiful rainfall, when everything would come to life. The grasslands would be so vast and so green, you could see easily for ten miles or more. The Shebelle River swelled, as all the little creeks and rivers flowed into it. By the time it reached our village, it was at least a hundred feet across or more. It was a source of life and renewal for all of us, even the animals – birds, monkeys, the jackals and hyenas, crocodiles, hippopotamus, even giraffe's would gather there. Everything teamed with life, as the forests and open areas blossomed with flowers and fruit and new growth. To me it was like living in a large park.

With the beauty of the rainy seasons and the harshness of the dry, came a peace, a calm, a quiet, that I have not enjoyed since I left there. The whole place, and all the villages around, and all the grasslands were free of cars, and buses, and trucks; there were no air conditioners humming in the background, no street lights to dim the stars at night, no TV's with their constant chatter and advertising. In fact, there was no electricity whatsoever for miles and miles around, until you reached Beledwayne, which was a good day's walk away.

Greatest of all, there were no clocks: clocks to tell you when to get up in the morning; clocks to watch all day long waiting for the end of the work day; clocks to remind you of how slowly the day is moving or how quickly; clocks to encourage you to wish the time away. There was only the sun and the moon and the stars, and from them, we scheduled our day. I really wasn't aware that a day had twenty four hours until I got older. We also didn't have any mail service or telephones or cell phones or computers. The only way to get word to one another in a different village or city, was to send your message with someone that was planning on going there, hoping they'd find the person you need to get hold of and give them the message. Also, no bills! My grandmother's hut and little farm and animals and food, everything, was paid for. And, if we couldn't pay for it, we simply didn't have it. I guess it's the simplicity of life I miss, when I think of the village. We had no clue of the struggles going on in the world, and even in our own country. Although, war did eventually reach us, at which time I saw my first white person.

Once I got a little older and well trained to herd the animals – cows included, a typical day for me, which was pretty much every day, meant getting up before sunrise when our alarm clock, the rooster, would wake me up. As soon as he crowed, I knew it was time to get off my wooden bed covered with a mat and get to work. Each day, I'd get up and quietly leave our hut so as not to disturb Grandma.

I'd wash my face outside in our cooking area, getting water from what was left in the water jugs, or "haans," that we kept under the trees and out of the sun. I'd brush my teeth with a stick about the size of a pencil cut from the branches of a Roomay tree. After soaking it in water, it becomes very fibrous making an excellent tooth brush.

I was always the first one up, as it was my job to start the early morning chores. I really enjoyed this time of day, as it was quiet in the village, and all the animals were still sleeping – very tranquil! I would watch the sun rise each morning, as I'd get the fire started, make a little breakfast, getting ready for the day's work, as the whole rest of the village slowly woke up as well. It was one of the most beautiful things I ever had the chance to witness – that first edge of dawn as it shyly peaked over the mountains. I still miss it to this day.

It was my job to get the fire going to make tea for our breakfast. I'd gather some wood from the wood pile and start a fire from the hot coals which still remained in the burning pit. We'd keep the ashes hot through the night by putting a good size log on the fire before going to bed, covering it with ashes and a pan on top to keep it just barely smoldering. Then in the morning, I'd take the pan off, throw on a few dry sticks and "pooff," the fire would be lit.

While everyone else enjoyed the tea, I'd make my meal, which would almost always be porridge made from corn grown in our fields. We'd keep the corn in a bag near the fire pit, so I'd take some and put it in a big wooden bowl called a "moye" made from the bottom of a tree trunk, all hollowed out. I'd add a little water, and with a long pole called a "kal," I'd pound it until it was all powdery and the inside of the corn would come loose from its shell. Then I'd pour it into a flat pan and toss it into the air, blowing on it to get the chaff out; I'd then leave it in the pan to let it dry in the open air.

While the corn was drying, I'd get our four "haans," or wooden water jugs. These were made from the skin of the Gaatir tree, which my grandmother would peel off the tree, soak in water, then make the haans. Each one held about four gallons of water. It took special skills to make them. I never did learn how to do it, and remember how Grandma was worried, that if I did not learn how to make a haans, how would I make a good wife and provide a home for my husband and children? Today I just turn on the faucet, and I still don't know how to make a haans! I'd have to wash them daily and heat them up by dropping hot cinders inside and twirling them around; this would get rid of any bacteria left in the residual water at the bottom from the day before.

Once done with getting the haans ready, I'd go get the strongest donkey from where he was fenced in, bring him out and tie him to a tree. First I'd put a grass 'filiq', or rug, on the donkey's back to protect him from the heaviness of the haans once filled with water, and then I'd hang two haans on each side of him and tighten the ropes together. Once ready, he and I would walk to the river which was about a mile away from our hut.

It was a nice walk through the village, with the smells of fires coming from neighbors and the sounds of animals and children moving about. The path down to the river was well trodden, as everyone in the village made it to the river at least once per day. It wove its way through some open land and fields, finally through the woods leading down to the river. There would be other girls walking their donkeys down to the river as well. We'd wave at each other and talk and visit, sometimes walking together.

The mornings were always so nice and cool and sometimes foggy. You could hear the birds and other animals down by the river - it was a nice time of the day. When I got there, I'd set the haans on the shore next to the river, let the donkey get a good long drink, then tie him to one of the trees, because if I didn't, he'd run away from me. So, I'd use a smaller jug to fill my haans with water and then lift each one onto the donkey's back one by one. Finally, I'd put their covers on and walk back home.

One particular morning, I walked with my aunt down to the river to get water for the day. It was a beautiful morning, the sun barely coming up, birds beginning their daily song, and everything nice and peaceful. We got to the river, and I went to the water's edge scooping up the water with my jug to fill the haans.

All of a sudden, my aunt started screaming, "Habibo, Habibo, get out of there, get out of there." I had no idea what she was talking about, as I was so busy scooping up water I didn't look around me. She kept on yelling and running towards me, "There's a crocodile, a crocodile, get out of there, hurry, get out of there." I looked up and there, right in front of me, maybe four feet away, were the eyes of a crocodile riding along as if on top of the water coming straight towards me; it was coming fast with a wake of water behind it. I stood straight up with more adrenaline pumping through me than I think I've ever had before or ever will have again. I let go of the water jug and fell backwards with my feet sinking into the muddy edge of the river. I quickly used my hands to and feet to pull myself backwards trying to scramble away from the water's edge. My aunt, by this time, was throwing things into the water at the crocodile and screaming. Crocodiles don't like a lot of screaming and commotion. She made as much noise as she could, and she was good at it, because the crocodile turned and went back into the river, but not without giving its prey - me - one last look with those two big eyes, as if saying, "Missed you this time, but be careful of the next." That's the day my eyes met those of a crocodile, and I hope it never happens again, because those are some pretty fearsome eyes to look into.

By the time I'd make it back to the village with my donkey, the sun would be coming up nicely over the mountains; it was always kind of orange and would illuminate the mountain peaks first and then pretty soon pop up on top of the mountains themselves like saying, "I'm in charge here." Walking back to the village, I'd see wisps of smoke coming up from the huts, and I could hear pots and pans rattling, cows starting to bellow and the goats and sheep bleating, calling to be fed.

Everyone would be pretty much awake at our place by the time I got back, so someone would usually help me take the haans off the donkey and put them in their spot under the tree to keep them out of the sun. Then, we'd let the donkeys loose. We had several, and we'd let them wander around outside the hero and through the village, grazing where ever they wanted, just like the other families would do with their donkeys. They'd stay close to home or wander around the village and usually come back on their own. If we needed to keep them close, or if we thought they'd run away, we'd tie their front legs together loosely, so they couldn't go too far. The males, especially, were very independent, and I'd usually have to go out before going to bed and find them – usually in someone else's hero or out in a grassy area grazing or just resting under a tree.

After getting water, and before milking the cows and goats, I'd let them out from within their fence and take them out to get some grass. If it was the dry season and no grass was available, we'd have some saved up hay they'd eat, and I'd give them some corn and oats that we'd keep stored away. I'd leave them out for about an hour to get their milk going, because once they've eaten, they'd have a much larger milk "let down." So, I'd bring them back into our hero, put them in their fence and let the baby cows suck the teet for awhile. After I'd take the calves away, I'd milk them. It would take me about an hour to milk ten goats and usually about six cows. I'd only get a few gallons, because the cows were always somewhat underfed and hungry and didn't give as much milk as those here in the States; plus, they'd have to feed the calves which took quite a bit of milk. We'd keep the milk inside the hut where it was cooler in a container called a "dhiil," lasting for a day or a little more. We'd drink it for our meals and use it to make butter by skimming the cream off the top, shaking it in a covered container until all of a sudden it separates from the butter milk and becomes butter.

After milking, I'd make my porridge out of the dried corn I let lay out in the open air, by cooking it in boiling water over the open fire. I'd add some goat's milk to make it thicker, a little cane sugar which we'd buy up in Beledewayne, and eat my breakfast, clean up the bowl and utensils, grab my walking stick and head out into the grasslands with the animals.

We'd wander out into the bush and be gone all day long with no food and no way of coming back home, because you don't dare bring the animals back until sunset, as they needed to graze for the whole day. We'd walk all day, but depending on the season, we may not have had to go too far, maybe several miles out. But in dry weather, we'd walk many, many miles, sometimes even as far as the mountains trying to find grass for them to eat.

We'd have four of these seasons per year, two rainy and two dry, so for three months I'd graze the animals close to home, then for three months I'd walk way out in the grasslands and so on. So, all day long the animals and I would pretty much be walking, and typically, I was just by myself with no one around for miles - just me and the cows.

The rainy season could be very difficult, as we still had to walk, even if it was pouring rain. A few kids actually died in the rain, as water would rise up to our knees very fast at times, and they'd be swept off their feet and drown. Some, from being wet and cold, would die from hypothermia.

A few times, I almost died out there as well. Depending on where the rain was coming from, the cows would always go in the opposite direction - if from the west they'd go east, if from the east they'd go west – and you have no choice but to stay with them. I would just follow until the rain stopped.

One time, because of the rain, I didn't get home until midnight. At that particular time, the rain came from the west where our village is, so the cows wanted to go in the opposite direction which took us to a wooded area. It was late in the evening when I was about ready to take them home, but the rain kept us from heading home as they wouldn't walk into it. So there I was, stuck in this woods in the heavy rain with my cows. I tried to stay under a tree, but it was so windy, I was afraid that the branches would fall on me. So, I sat outside in the rain beside one of the cows. I was so cold, that I started to shiver and couldn't keep myself together much longer. To get something warm in me, I went to one of my favorite cows and got some warm milk - I have to say that helped a bit. After a while, the rain stopped, but it was already dark; so I took my dress off and squeezed all the water out and walked the cows' home as if nothing had ever happened. Needless to say, I was happy to be home, even if home was a hut. I slept very well that night.

Each day, every day, by the time the sun was a little past its peak, and if I was close enough to the village, of course, and not way out in the grasslands, I would take the herd to the river for their water and their rest. This part of the day was always a good time for me, as I'd get to swim and bathe in the river, wash my hair, and get all the dust and dirt off me. The animals liked it, too. They'd drink to their heart's content, even walk in the water to cool off – and I was right in there with them – swimming amongst them! After cleaning up and cooling down, we'd take our little siesta, resting by the river in the shade, and enjoy the quiet.

We'd finish the day by going back out to the grasslands, probably around 2:00 in the afternoon, to wander around, or I'd just sit under a tree and let the animals graze. Sometimes, I'd play around by myself or with some other kids if there were some in the area. It was nice to be able to sit out there with nothing but grasslands extending for many miles with the mountains off in the background, the sheep and goats or cows contentedly grazing. I'd often just stare off towards the mountains, wondering what was on the other side, as I'd never been past them. I sometimes fantasized that maybe I'd marry and have a nice home with children and live in a safe place. Oddly enough, that fantasy came true!

As the sun started to go down, it would be time to go home. I'd whistle my special whistles calling the herd, and they knew just exactly what we were to do – time to go home for the night! As the herd got closer to the village, they'd start to recognize the way, so they'd lead me rather than me leading them. They'd all go into their pen, happy to be home and content from a day of grazing and walking, tired from the walk, just as I was. After milking the goats and the cows, my day of chores was finished once again.

I'd usually prepare some corn or barley for our supper, grinding it, then cooking it over the fire. By this time Ahmed was home, as was my grandmother from their day of work grazing the herd of goats and sheep, or working out in the fields, which Ahmed would do quite often. I remember what a peaceful time this was, with the sun already past the mountains in the west, and all the night insects and creatures making their music. We'd sit around the fire on the ground sometimes talking about things that happened during the day, other times we'd just sit and eat silently all tired from the day's work.

After our supper, I would have to go find the donkeys, because they'd be needed early in the morning to go get water. So, I'd start my evening ritual of wandering around the village, stopping to visit along the way, and eventually find them somewhere. Here's where I could walk through the village checking out the neighbors, chatting with a few kids my age along the way, getting caught up on some of the news in the village. Eventually, I would find the donkeys and bring them back home. I'd tie them to a little tree, so they'd be ready to get water in the morning or for their work if Ahmed needed them. Finally, I'd go fall on my mat in the hut and fall asleep immediately. And, in the morning, the rooster would crow at 4:30 or 5:00 waking me up, and it would all start over again!

Now that I'm older, I realize how our environment shapes us into who we are. I learned to enjoy being alone with the herd, and I learned how to entertain myself for days on end all by myself. When I could be with others, that was great, however, most of the time, I was a loner, as I still am to a certain degree.

My life is so different here in America, working as a nurse, living in a comfortable home with TV's and computers and cell phones, I have trouble with feelings of not really knowing where I fit in. A very large part of me is still that village girl out herding the animals or swimming in the river, yet another side of me is a "modernized" woman, having learned English and the American culture, driving a car, shopping in the malls, being a nurse in a large institution in a bustling city in America. I imagine if I had a pair of sandals made out of old tires and a cloth wrapped around me carrying a long walking stick, I'd feel very much at home. Sometimes I feel that perhaps I'm behind others, as my girlfriends will talk about fashions or purses and girly things, and I really don't know what they're talking about, much less understand it. I guess I'm still a village girl happy to have a dress or two and a decent pair of shoes – not made out of tires!

I see that I am who I am today, because of the work I had to do as a young girl. From the age of five, I had to be on high alert herding the animals and watching for jackals or hyenas, rapists or crocodiles that all wanted a piece of the flock, or sometimes a piece of me. I always had to be on my guard. And, I've forgiven the ill-treatment inflicted on me, as the perpetrators were young, the culture was flawed, and everyone has moved on in their lives.

My son, Mohamed, got up this morning and wanted cereal, so, I asked him what he'd like. His biggest problem was choosing from the five different kinds in the cupboard. He didn't want this one, and he didn't want that one, and he didn't like that other one. Sometimes I think to myself that my children need to live in the village for a few years without the tremendous amount of good things they enjoy right now. However, life there was rough, very rough! So, I try to tell my children to appreciate what they have, and to remember that they have to work for that. Sometimes I'll remind my daughter how I had it as a young girl, and her response is usually, "Yea, yea, yea, mom, I know all those stories."

I'm very thankful that I can provide enough for my children that they never have to worry about where their next meal is coming from, and that they can go to the refrigerator and choose grapes or oranges or apples or a glass of milk. And they don't have to wonder if they're going to get beaten up and raped today or not! My heart goes out to those that are still living that way, only having one meal a day if they're fortunate, or living in fear – such as those still suffering in Dadaab or in the villages of Somalia.

My favorite things to do now are to read books, anything in the sciences. I like to learn new things; I listen to NPR a lot, as I enjoy finding out what's going on in the world. Perhaps being raised with no word from the outside world, in fact, I didn't even know there was an outside world, gave me a strong desire to learn more about it and be a part of it. But in this fast world, it's very important to also sit by the river under a tree and have some rest and quiet time all by one's self!

I look back now on the many, many hours and days I'd be all by myself. Sometimes I long for some quiet moments, as I seem to have multiple things on my plate most of the time as a wife, mother, working nurse, and student. I learned at a very young age, to appreciate the quiet and the peace of being by myself. In this busy world we live in, that, to me, is a luxury to be treasured which few people get to enjoy.

Chapter Six

Malaria

———•••———

I had malaria so many times in my life that I lost count after 12 – and survived. Growing up out in the bush country, getting malaria was the same as getting the common cold here in the USA. It was a household term, and each year it would take its toll on the whole African population. The World Health Organization has labeled it as the main child killer on the continent. In the villages and out in the country, with all the standing water and ponds during the two rainy seasons, malaria runs rampant carried by all the mosquitoes. In fact, we would consider ourselves lucky if we did not catch malaria, and would hope we didn't catch it the next season.

Often when we had malaria, we would let it run its course per se, because there was no access to medication or vaccinations outside the main cities, so we couldn't prevent it or fight it. We just let it runs its course and hoped for the best that we could beat the bouts of fever. We had no screens over the doors to our huts and no mosquito mesh over where we'd sleep. It was kind of like we held up a big sign saying, "I'm full of blood, please come and bite me even if you're carrying malaria."

Sadly, though, I saw many die from it in our village. It's a terrible disease with, what we called, the shaking chills, as your fever gets so high that, first you go out of your mind, and secondly, you burst into sweat and chills – day after day. I remember seeing so many times, bodies of relatives and friends taken outside the village to an area designated for burial with no headstones or footstones or even names to mark their graves.

One of the worst bouts for me happened in 1989 when I was about eight. It was the rainy season and mosquitoes were everywhere – down by the river, in the ponds, out in the grasslands, even in our own cow yard – everywhere! Well, I got bitten - again, and within a few days I was sick - really sick! With malaria, your fever runs high, and you become very chilled with extremely strong shakes. It seems like the trademark of malaria is the shaking chills and fever that brings you right out of your head. My fever ran to at least 105 degrees and would spike and drop and spike again, over and over. Dehydration sets in very quickly, and soon I couldn't even walk from being so weak.

I spent my days lying in the hut on my little mat covering my wooden bed, covered with a thin blanket, because I had the shaking chills from my fever. Sometimes to get into the warm air, I'd lie out under the big tree where my uncle, Ahmed slept. I couldn't eat or drink much, my fever ran very high, and most of the time I was in a state of delirium. After a week or so, my grandma even sent my uncle, Abdi, to Beledwayne to purchase some medications for malaria, but even that did not cure my illness. Many times, the medications in Somalia are expired and would not do anything for you.

After a month or so into malaria, it did not rain well in our village, so my grandmother and Ahmed decided that we had to move our animals far out into the grasslands to graze them for a few months, which meant living again as nomads in order to keep the animals alive like we had to do several times before. They decided to take me along with them, with the hopes that I'd get better and be able to help them herd the animals.

My grandma and Ahmed got all the animals ready to go and gathered together the main belongings that would be needed for survival, and packed them onto the donkey cart, as I lay sick in the hut or under the tree. This is one of the benefits of being sick, as I didn't have to do anything. Early the next morning, they loaded me on top of the big pile of belongings we were taking along - pots, pans, food, water jugs, utensils, branches and rugs to build a hut, and a few of the essentials of life that we'd need for at least three months out in the grasslands - and the clothes we brought was what we had on our backs! So that's where I rode on a little makeshift bed with a blanket as we made our way through the very dry and very dusty grasslands formerly verdant with green growth. We slowly walked, perhaps twenty five miles per day to get to the grassy areas that were still having some rain. We took all the cows – about forty in all, seventy five sheep and goats, as well three donkeys to take turns pulling the cart with me on top. Grandma walked up front leading the herd, while Ahmed handled the donkey cart from behind.

We left the village and walked about a half a day, and rested for the night throwing together a make-shift hut with a few branches and rugs thrown over them. Grandma would cook a little porridge, which I couldn't eat. I just lay in the hut and shivered. We traveled again the next day for half a day, rested half a day, then went again the next day and so on for several days.

I remember being so glad I was sick, so I didn't have to walk, because that walking just kills you; your feet hurt so bad, you're tired and so hot and you can't stop. It's not just the walking, it's keeping the animals in place, too, so you don't lose any, and if one of them is not able to walk, you help them; if one gets lazy and sits down, you have to get it up and moving; if one tries to run away, you run after it with your walking stick and bring it back. You can get so tired, that you can't hardly walk anymore. You walk, walk and walk and always in a state of hunger.

I spent most of the time in a state of delirium, seeing things that weren't there, thinking crazy things. My grandmother was so worried about me because that was the sickest she had ever seen me. She told me, years later, that I would wake up in the middle of the night and walk around hallucinating and talking nonsense because of my high fever. I feel bad that she had to worry about me as well as the animals. I don't remember much of the experiences; sometimes I remember the bloody showers.

Because we had the donkey and cart, we had to travel using some of the paths that meandered through the open grasslands made by other nomads that went before us. After the third day of walking, all of a sudden it started getting greener and greener and the animals began their grazing as they were very hungry from the walk without having much food.

Grandma and Ahmed found an abandoned camp where nomads had been before us, and they decided to stop there to set up our camp. It was a good spot, out in the open where they could watch the herd, and there was already a makeshift frame for a hut and a corral with branches and brush to keep the animals in at night. Nomads using and leaving sites like this after one another is very common, and that's just what nomads do. You'd never find any utensils or anything useful left behind as they're too precious.

I spent most of the time by myself in the little makeshift hut Grandma and Ahmed made. Ahmed would take the cows, and Grandma the goats and sheep, out to graze each day at sunup and return just as the sun was going down. I would just lay there by myself and have some water to drink and a little porridge in the morning - that was if I could eat anything at all. Sometimes Grandma would put porridge in a little bowl for me to eat later on in the day which I would try to eat to keep up my strength. I would just lie there shivering and shaking, hallucinating, not even sure where I was. If I could, I'd get outside the hut and lay in the hot sun under my blanket because it made me feel better being always chilled and shaking and my teeth rattling. I remember how the heat felt so good. Plus, being out in the sun is one of the ways to kill the malaria bacteria. Over a three month period, I got so sick that I lost about twenty pounds, was unable to eat and could barely drink water. This is one of the times my grandmother soaked tobacco and gave me the juice. What a disgusting taste. I remember it was so bitter. I was so high after that and feeling so much better, I started to walk around.

One of the main home remedies the villagers, and my grandmother, used to try to cure malaria was to wash the sick person with warm animal blood and leave it on for twenty four hours. Several times I had to endure this, having had malaria so many times in my life. I hated the smell of the blood, and I still hate it. I probably don't need to tell you that this does not work, it's a folk medicine. However, it was believed to help for some reason.

Well, sure enough, after about a week of being out in the grasslands, we had a goat that got sick and was dying. Bless their hearts, Grandma and Ahmed decided to slaughter it and use its blood to bathe me in. So, Ahmed cut the goat's throat, and Grandma helped to catch all the blood in a large wooden bowl. I saw it coming and thought, "Oh, my, please don't let this happen to me again." Then, Grandma took my clothes off and laid me on the grass and took the warm blood and poured it on me rubbing it everywhere all over my body – in my hair, on my face, my legs and arms, my chest and stomach, all over my back and back side, my ears, eyelashes, eyebrows – everywhere! And she rubbed it into my skin. I hate blood to this day because of that. After she rubbed it on and in, I had to go back into the hut and cover up with my blanket.

The blood dried on me, and I had to sleep with it on. I kept it on for twenty four hours, and as you can imagine, it got real sticky and crusty and smelly. The hut smelled like a slaughter house, and I had nothing to keep the flies and bugs off me and was too weak to even care. Then the next day, Grandma carried me down to the pond where she washed if all off with pond water. Needless to say, I did not get better, but, Grandma and Ahmed tried the best they could to help me, and I'm thankful for that.

Before too long, the animals grazed as much as they could from that area, so, like nomads do, we had to move again to find more grazing for them. Grandma and Ahmed packed up our belongings and me, and we headed out. By this time, I was getting sicker and sicker - throwing up, constant shaking chills, cold sweats. We didn't know it at the time, but my cousin, Farhiyo, caught malaria and was also about seven and living in the village as well, she passed away from the disease.

We traveled from our camp up in the mountains to a new site back down in the valley near a small village where the grass was green and yet ungrazed. That's when my grandmother decided that she should get in contact with my mother to see if she could take me to Mogadishu to get some medical help. She asked around the little village that we were near if anyone was going to Mogadishu and found a man that was going the next day; so she asked him to go find my mother telling her to come for me. She told him the area that my mother lived in, and asked him to hurry to tell her that I was sick and she needed to come and take me to a hospital, otherwise I might get to a point of no recovery and die. So, the man went to Mogadishu and the area that my grandmother told him my mother was living in and asked around if anyone knew where Khadija was living. Soon, he found where she was, and gave her the message. I owe my life to that man. Had he delayed or not given the message to my mother, I would not be telling this story today.

My mother left Mogadishu as soon as she could, taking the bus as far as she could and then walking the remaining miles to the little village we were camped next to. The people in the village told her how to get to where we were in the grasslands outside the village.

I remember, it was late in the afternoon, maybe around 5:00 pm, with some daylight still remaining. I was lying under a large tree all by myself, while grandma and Ahmed were still out with the animals. I was covered with a small blanket just lying there when I saw my mother walking toward me out of the bushes. I thought maybe I was hallucinating, as I hadn't seen her in several years. But, it was her. I was so excited just seeing her appearance that I wanted to get up and run toward her so I could embrace her and give her a hug; but, as soon as I tried to get up, I collapsed to the ground being extremely weak. Eventually, she reached me and bent down to hold me and gave me a big hug.

I remember her telling me everything was going to be alright, and that she was going to take me to a hospital so I could get some medicine and feel better. Can you imagine what that would feel like seeing one of your parents that you have not seen in a such a long time, maybe three years earlier, walking toward you and not being able to run or walk toward them to embrace them, or that he or she would put their arms around you and pick you up. She set me down and took care of me, giving me sips of water, carrying me into the hut, cleaning me off from all my sweat.

After sleeping in the hut that night right next to me, my mother took me the very next day, early in the morning, to catch the bus. Of course, we had to make the journey through the bush to the main road, her carrying me, as I couldn't walk. We were lucky to catch a ride from someone who was going half way to where we were to catch the bus, so we rode on his donkey cart. Then, the man let us down because he was going a different way, and we still had about fifteen miles to go. So my mother picked me up and carried me on her back with my legs around her waist and arms around her neck. A few times she had to sit down and rest as she's a small woman, about 5'2" but pretty strong and about twenty four years old at the time. Once we arrived at the bus station, we had to wait several hours for the bus to arrive. So I lay on the ground with my blanket, and my mother bought some tea with milk for me to drink because I was not able to eat any solid food.

Finally, the bus arrived, and we were able to board. This was my first time being on any kind of a motorized vehicle, and as soon as the bus drove away I began to get car sick. The bus had seats which faced each other, and that's how we had to sit. I was trying to hold it together as much as I could, but finally I just had to let it out, and, in the process, ended up vomiting on my mother and the lady sitting across from us. My mother said, "Habiba! Why didn't you tell me you were going to vomit, I could have given you a bag?" I told her, "I was afraid." And then she said, "I'm your mother, and you should not be afraid of me."

After I vomited, I half dozed off to sleep in a feverish, half conscious state, not waking until we got to Mogadishu - about a six hour drive. We got off the bus and took a taxi to my mother's apartment. When we got out of the taxi, I could not believe what I was seeing. It was the biggest and tallest building I had ever seen. It was at least eight stories tall; I couldn't believe they made such structures. My mother lived on the 5th floor in an apartment that had 3 bedrooms and one bathroom. When we got there, she gave me a shower. I had never taken a shower before in my life having only washed up in the river or ponds near the village. I couldn't eat, I just said, "No, I just want to lie down because I'm so extremely exhausted." She took me to a beautiful room with a big bed, nice thick blanket, sheets which I had never lain on before, Oh, and a pillow. That was the first time I had ever seen any of these things, and that was so exciting to me. Having come from living and sleeping in a hut about eight feet in diameter with no windows, sleeping on a bed made of logs shaved flat with a thin mat laid on top and an old cloth for a pillow, from cooking meals outside on rocks and when grazing the animals sleeping on the ground, I felt like I died and went to live in the palace of a queen. My mother lived there with her husband and no kids. Right then I decided I was going to stay there with her and not return to my grandma's village as there was plenty of room for me. This made me glad that I was so sick because I had never been in such a nice place in all my life.

The next day, my mother took me to the hospital, and they did some blood and stool tests. They found out that I indeed did have malaria as well as a parasitic infection in my stomach and was severely anemic. So, I had to be on four different medications, and had to be given injections in my hips twice a day for three weeks. The doctor sent me back home, and I had to return to the hospital each morning and afternoon every day for three weeks to receive the injections. Can you imagine being eight years old and having forty two injections within three weeks? And, they were big needles! It's a bit traumatizing, if you ask me. I also had to be on oral medications. Mother could not get me to swallow the large pills, as they were so bitter. As a result of the many injections I had to receive, my hips became swollen and blew up like a soft ball, and one of the injection sites on my right hip got infected. I remember my mom used to ice it a few times each day. Unfortunately, it created sciatic nerve problems in my right hip. I wonder if they even knew what a sciatic nerve was in that hospital.

After the first two weeks of treatment, I began to feel better. Each day, I'd sit on my mother's balcony and gaze through the railing to watch the kids that were playing down below on the dirt street. They would play soccer for hours; I couldn't believe that they were doing nothing with their time but playing for hours and hours with no chores or anything else to do. I thought, "How could those kids have free time like that and how lucky they were." So I asked my mother if I could go play with them, and she said that I was still too sick to go play outside, but I could watch them from the balcony.

After I completed my treatment and felt a lot better, my mother allowed me to go play with those kids. We played stuff I didn't even know how to play. They didn't really like me because city kids and country kids don't mix together very well. They could tell by how I spoke that I was from the country. Their language was a little more refined, whereas mine was more crude.

Sometimes my mother would let me go grocery shopping for her. I remember her taking me for shopping for a new dress and sandals. I asked her, "What are those for, because I have lots of clothes already - maybe two pair? I thought that was extravagant. I remember my mother taking me shopping for a new ambuuer, or long dress, and sandals. Then I asked my mother what are those for, because I have lots of clothes already - maybe two pair. Because when I lived with grandmother in the village, all I had was one dress.

So mom told me that we are going to visit your dad tomorrow, I said, "Oh really, you're not joking with me about this?" And she said, "Yes, yes that is the truth." I was so happy that I was going to see my father, that I could not sleep. I tossed and turned all night and just couldn't wait until the next morning, because I wanted to be ready and out the door pretty early. I woke my mom up at 7:00 am thinking that we were going to leave soon, but mom was like we need to go in the afternoon, because we never visit anyone in the morning. By three in the afternoon people in Somalia are done with their daily business and stay home after that. I waited patiently, and then two o'clock arrived. I was so impatient that day so I ended up asking my mother countless times, "Hoyo (mom), is it time to leave yet?"

Finally, mom and I left. We had to walk for about a half a mile to get to the bus station; we boarded the bus, and it took us about 30 minutes to get there. We had to walk a few blocks to get to my dad's house; it was a blue house with a brown gate for the entrance. He and his second wife lived there with their four children. As we entered the gate, one of my little sisters ran up to us and asked who we were, and then it was my stepmother and my two other sisters and brother that all came out to say hello to us. My mom left me after a few minutes and said that she will be back in two days' time. I was so happy that I was there at my dad's house.

I asked my step mother several times when my dad was going to come home as the evening wore on. She told me not to wait up because he was not coming anytime soon; and of course my dad did not get there until we were all asleep. When I woke up the next morning, I went to my dad's room and saw that he has left for the day. I was really sad, I actually cried in the bathroom. The whole day seemed like years, because all I wanted was to see my dad. Next morning, I woke up very early and walked into his room there I saw him sleeping. I ran up to his bed to say hello to him; he gave me a hug and told me that I had grown and that it was good to see me. He had to go back to sleep so I came out and played with my little sisters. That was the first times as a child I seen my father and the last time I seem him.

Sometimes a lot of my sadness and anger comes from not having my father in my life. I longed so long for a relationship with my father. I have always felt the outcast in the family from my father's side, partially maybe because it's true. A child needs, especially girls, need her father in her life. Otherwise how is she supposed to know what is acceptable in a relationship or not. A father is supposed to show you tenderness, love and is supposed to show you how a man should treat you. What people need to understand is that when two people get divorced you are still responsible for the child. I wished and hope many times that my father would walk through the bush and would walk into our hero and bring me presents, which never happened. This broke my heart over and over, again and still does in some ways. Sometimes I wonder how I would have turn out had I grew up with my dad.

Before too long, my mother told me I had to go back to the village. My heart just sank. I was having so much fun - fun I had never been able to have before. I felt so happy to have friends to play with, and living with my mother felt so wonderful. I pretended to be sick, because I didn't want to go back. I was afraid to tell her I didn't want to go back; I just wasn't comfortable telling her. I mainly wanted to be around her and did not want to go back to the work and harsh environment with my grandma in the village. She said, "Oh, I think you're OK and able to go." My heart just sank. I couldn't understand why I was not able to stay with her especially since she had so much room and seemed to have enough money to take care of me. I thought about the other children playing outside and wished so badly that I could be like one of them, living with their parents, having friends, going to school. Instead, I knew what waited for me back at the village – no affection, criticism, work every single day with no days off. So I said, "Well, if I'm going, I want to take a present for my grandmother." I knew there was only one thing that would make my grandma happy – sugar! She liked it better than gold. So my mother bought five kilos of sugar and a few bags of black tea which we bought in bulk. My mother also helped me buy a bottle of sesame oil, a pair of shoes for my uncle Ahmed, and a dress for my grandma.

I expected my mother to come with me to the village, but instead, she brought me to the bus station in Mogadishu early one morning, put me on the bus and said good bye. I was so nervous. I pleaded with her to come with me, but she said she couldn't. I was sick to my stomach with fear and worried I would throw up on the bus like I did on the way there. I remember the whole time wondering why can't I stay, am I not good enough, doesn't she love me or want me? I felt rejected.

I reluctantly boarded the bus and sat next to a lady going in the same direction as me. She was very kind to me on the trip which lasted about six hours. She asked why I was traveling and why no one was with me. I explained that I was going back to my grandmother's village, Balcad, and my mother couldn't come; she was very surprised I was traveling alone. She was so kind, giving me some fruit which I sparingly ate for fear of throwing up, and she comforted me.

The bus got to Trejenta, about seventeen miles from Balcad in the early evening. We both got off the bus, she was heading south, I had to go north. I had way too much to carry – ten pounds of sugar, packages with shoes and a dress, a bottle of oil, tea, along with the items my mother bought for me. The lady I traveled with said, "Why did you bring all this?" I said, "My grandma likes tea, so when I get home I can make tea with sugar for her." All was too heavy to carry along, so the lady spoke to the shopkeeper at the bus stop, asking if I could leave my items there. He was OK with that, so I just carried the sugar and tea with me, and left the rest there. The lady told me to take care of myself and to be careful walking home and then went on her way. So, there I was, seven years old standing by myself at a little out of the way bus stop in the middle of the Somali grasslands.

I walked the seventeen miles, even though my hips were still very sore from all the shots I got at the hospital. I remember it was getting dark, and from experience grazing the animals, I knew the night animals were coming out soon – hyenas in particular! I recalled that four months earlier a young girl about ten years old was attacked and raped along this very path, and she did not survive it. That's all I could think of as I walked along the path, nightfall coming quickly, and I still had quite a ways to walk. I pretty much knew the way and some of the short cuts through the bushes walking as quickly as I could. However, I was still not feeling very well from my struggle with malaria. I tried to stay mainly in the open land, but at times the path went through wooded areas and very remote places and around farmer's fields. It was the dry season, so there was nothing green, and the path was pretty well worn.

When I got home it was dark. From a distance, I could see the village with some fires burning outside people's huts, and soon I could hear the sounds of animals and people as I got closer. I came to our hut, and I was so glad to see that my Grandma was there. She gave me a hug and said, "Oh, you look so good, you've gained weight and you've got chubby cheeks." We hugged, and I said, "I brought you sugar and tea, Grandma." She said, "Oh, you know what I like." I told her I left the rest of the gifts at the bus station, because I couldn't carry them, so my dear Uncle Ahmed, the next day, walked back and got the rest from the store owner.

Right away, I was back to my responsibilities. That very evening I did my chores and prepared for the next morning, when I would have to take the goats and sheep out to graze. And, my routine began again! At that point I was really upset at my mother, and I was hoping somehow I would end up with bad malaria again so that I could go back to my Mogadishu and stay with my mother.

A few weeks later due to the terribly dry weather, we had to move again out into the grasslands to graze the animals. So, Grandma, Ahmed and I took all the cows and sheep and goats and headed out. This time, I could not ride on the donkey cart, but had to walk alongside the animals to help keep them in line. Through the whole journey, my thoughts went back to my mother's home. I couldn't stop thinking about the nice bed, the sheets and pillows, running water, and the children playing. Most of all, though, my thoughts went to my mother, and how much I wished I had her in my life so that I could be like the rest of the children. But, I walked alongside the animals, dust wafting through the air from their hooves, through the parched and dry countryside, looking for green grass. I thought to myself, "They are my family and loved ones, and this was my life."

Chapter Seven

Field Work

———•◦•———

From early on, there was no opportunity for me to go to school. Actually, there were no schools in our little village at all. There was, of course, a little bit of schooling, not like math and sciences and English which were for the boys, but teaching from the Quran. We girls weren't allowed to be educated, because girls were to stay at home cooking and cleaning and looking after the goats, sheep and cows; and by the time girls turned fourteen, we were expected to be married and have babies and that's it; there was no other possibility for our lives. Same situation is still true for the girls living in the village.

I was the only helper my grandma and uncles had, so I worked where I was needed, which meant helping with spring planting and fall harvesting. I resented that others could have time to relax and take a break, like my uncles or grandmother or the other kids in the village, but I didn't have that luxury. I had no time off. Girls would normally do the milking, cooking, and preparing the food that the men and boys would bring in from the fields. But I did the work of both, not only preparing food for us to eat, but also doing the work in the fields as well as the grazing of the animals. I never really said much about it or complained, like "I don't want to do this or don't want to do that." I couldn't really say that, but inside to myself I would say, "Oh God, is this really all there is to life?" In Somali culture, if you were asked to do something by someone older than yourself, you never complained or questioned, you just did it! You never would say no.

One of the harder chores I had to do was planting and harvesting the barley crops. However, now that I look back, I would love to be out in those fields one more time enjoying the sunshine, the company of my uncle Ahmed - who I miss so much, and the companionship of the other young people of the village. Barley was the main crop that everyone in the village grew, as it was the main staple for our food – we'd cook it into porridge, mix it in with beans and olive oil for our dinners, and just use it daily. It was never used for the animals, as they had the grass to eat and sometimes some corn.

We'd plant according to the seasons, of course, there being four in Somalia; two of the seasons are rainy and two are dry and harsh. The main rainy season, called Gu, occurs from April to June, and this is when everything turns green - even the desert. The second rainy season, called Dayr, occurs from October through December. Gu is like the Spring with plenty of rain and nice green grass. Dayr occurs later in the fall and starts very dry then slowly the rains begin again. The other two seasons, Xagaa which is like winter and lasts from December to March, is very dry and the weather is harsh; and Jiilaal, which lasts from July through September, is very, very dry and hot. However, being only about 400 miles north of the equator, the weather is always warm. The two rainy seasons usually allowed us to plant our barley twice – once in April and again in October.

North of the village was a large area of many acres which was divided up amongst the various families: some had an acre or two, others had quite a few acres, with most of the land having been handed down from one generation to the next always staying in the family. However, some families would purchase more land as it became available. My grandmother and uncles owned about seven acres which we'd plant every year - hopefully twice. I was the only girl in our village that would help to plant the corn and barley, as normally this was a for the boys and men of the village. But, for us, I was the main helper. Usually it was my uncle, Ahmed and I who would do the planting, sometimes my grandma would help, but, most of the time, as we were planting, she would take over grazing the animals for the morning or the whole day until I came back from the field work.

After the first rain of the year, all the villagers would go out to their farming plots to plant their barley. Ahmed and I would go out to the fields early in the morning. We'd gather the things we needed, like a long pole for him to poke holes in the ground, a burlap bag of barley seed for me to carry, some water, and maybe a little boiled corn. We'd walk the mile or so to the fields – usually about a half hour walk which I really enjoyed, as I'd be able to spend time with Ahmed. I remember so well how we'd walk in the cool of the morning, everything so nice and quiet and the village barely waking up, many times fog hanging around in the lower areas. As we walked the path to the fields, we'd talk about lots of things - the animals, the other people in the village, even about my other uncles and grandma and what they were up to. Ahmed was, and still is, a very tall man, about six feet four inches. He worked hard all the time and was very strong and lean with very dark skin. He was so kind and thoughtful with a beautiful smile and dark eyes. He only said what he meant, never raised his voice and encouraged me often in a very tender way. My time spent with him was very nice, and, if it weren't for him, my life in the village would have been very harsh, but he added warmth to my life. With the mountains in the distance and the cool morning air refreshing us, it was a nice walk and a welcome break for me from grazing the animals.

The fields in planting time are all open and bare from the last season's crop. We wouldn't plow them or cultivate them, because after each harvest, we'd take our animals out there and let them graze in the fields, and they'd eat down all the leftover stalks and rubble and work up the land with their hooves. There weren't any fences between the people's fields, only bushes which everyone would let grow so that they'd make a border.

To plant the fields, Ahmed would walk along with his long stick and poke it in the ground to open a hole, then, from the burlap bag hanging over my shoulder, I would throw a few barley seeds into the hole and close it over with my feet. So on we'd go, down one long row then make our way back the next row, then down again and back again until the whole field was planted, usually getting a couple acres planted in a day. It was fun with Ahmed as he and I could talk about anything. He had such a soothing gentle voice. He wasn't really super talkative, so we would just talk about random things. Sometimes, we would just plant in silence and enjoy the sunshine and each other's company. Several times we'd take a break and go sit on a little hill or somewhere where it was dry and not wet like the fields; we'd eat some of the food we brought along or just have some water and enjoy the quiet.

When the planting was all finished, we'd leave the fields alone for a month or so until the barley plants were about six inches high. Then, Ahmed and I, once again, would walk along all the rows and hoe them, getting all the grass and weeds out of the rows and away from the small plants, taking a good several days to finish it all. I remember Ahmed saying I was like a boy and did such a good job to get all the weeds and roots out. It was a big job out in the sun, and our hands would get blistered and sore. However, it had to be done or we'd lose the crop, and I was proud that I could do a good job and work like a boy, because we didn't have a boy - we had me! We only had to go through the fields hoeing once, after that, we just let the crop grow until it was time to harvest.

Some people lived near the village who were Bantu by origin. They were of a different tribe than us and lived on the opposite side of the river. Many of them were poor, like migrant workers that work the fields for farmers in other countries. So, some families, if they could afford it, would hire them to come and help do the hoeing. We couldn't mix with them as they were from a different tribal lineage, but many times we'd play with them when we were at the river, as they'd be playing on the opposite side of the river; but, being from a different tribe we could never have thought of marrying one. If one of our girls married a Bantu, she would be cut off from our tribe forever. Unfortunately, it was all a pride thing - racism, just like in other societies where people are not accepted because of their heritage or ethnicity or color of their skin or that they're different from us – such a basic human problem, isn't it? Sadly, many times the animals are less prejudiced than us humans; I guess we haven't progressed that much past them, have we?

One of the families that lived in the village owned a large water pump which was submerged permanently in the river. If the weather was dry, which it often was, the other families would pay them to pump the river water to irrigate their fields. The canals between the fields were dug many years ago: a deep canal was dug from the river to the fields and then smaller canals to each individual field in a big zig zag pattern. The water would be pumped into the big canal, and then whoever wanted the water for their fields would divert it their way through the smaller canals and soak their field. Flooding the fields was no small task, however. It was a big job with lots of digging and directing of the water, closing off channels to some fields by piling up mounds of dirt in the canals and opening them to another.

Each season Ahmed and I, as well as friends of his, would work hard to divert the water. I, once again, was the only girl that helped do this kind of work. Because of it, I became very comfortable working with boys and men, and to this day find it easier making friends with males versus females. Men don't seem to get too deep, whereas girls and women get all emotional about their husbands or boyfriends, their kids, and their feelings, and in the end someone always gets their feelings hurt, and then the friendship gets very dramatic. Men aren't like that, and I appreciate that about them. They were very good to work with, even if the work was hard, and they treated me with respect and praised me for a job well done. Perhaps we women need to take a lesson from the men and give them the respect they deserve rather than criticizing them!

When the barley was about five feet tall and the seed pod on top came out with a large bunch of seeds on it, all the birds would come around and try to eat the seeds. They thought, "Great, harvest time!" So, Ahmed and I would build a stand made of three strong, six-foot poles dug into the ground with a platform on the top and a ladder leading up to it. At the same time, all the other families were building their stands, as the birds would eat the fields clean if they could. Then, I and the young boys from each family would sit on those stands and keep the birds away by using a sling shot made out of a long rope with a pouch in the middle and a small loop on one end. We'd hold both ends in one hand, putting the loop around our little finger and a rock in the pouch. After twirling the sling around our head very fast and letting go of one end of it, the rock would fly out and scare the birds away. Everyone said I could do it like a boy, and I guess the truth is that I could do it like a boy, and the rocks I'd throw would really go far. I guess this is how David killed Goliath!

It was my job in our family to sit on the stand all day long - every single day - for about a month and work to keep the birds away. We could see each other sitting around the fields, each one on their stand throughout the open barley fields slinging rocks at the birds. I was usually the only girl out there in the middle of these fields, and as I got older, I'd have lots of fun interacting with the boys who were about my age. It was a fun time, sitting out there in the sunshine, waving at each other, seeing how good you could get with the sling shot. And, for treats, we'd all sit out there and chew on the stalks of the barley as it was sweet and full of juice. It was at this time that I started to discover that I liked boys – and they liked me. I started to awaken to the fact that I was becoming a young woman and soon, hopefully, would have a family of my own. This got me thinking about having my own place and being more of my own boss rather than my grandma or uncles.

This was a very social time for young people in the village. Many times we'd build a little fire, then grill some of the barley ends on it and eat them. Sometimes we'd yell to a friend close to us to watch our field so we could go visit with one another. It was a beautiful setting with trees scattered throughout, mountains in the distance, the barley fields full and almost ripe, young people scattered around the fields sitting on stands, little bonfires here and there, and rocks being hurled by sling shots, and being in the Fall of the year, it was cool and usually with nice breezes. Someday, maybe I can teach my two daughters how to use a sling shot like a boy!

Harvest would finally come at the end of the season when the seed pods were fully ripe. This was always great fun and a very busy time of the year for the whole village. Ahmed and I would again gather all the supplies we'd need and head out to the fields. We'd go through and chop all the barley down with a machete and gather it in armfuls putting it in piles all along the rows as we made our way through the field. It would take several days to get it all cut and laid out in piles.

Once finished, we'd put the barley in stand up piles like corn stacks with the pods on top and cover them with large leaves to protect them from the birds. We'd let them stand there and dry in the fields for a few weeks. It was a pretty sight all the stands of barley scattered across the fields kind of like corn would be stood to dry in the old days of America and other countries.

After a week or so, the stacks of barley would be dry from standing in the sun. So, we'd lay them down in circles with the heads facing into the middle of the circle. By the time we were done, we'd have quite a few of these barley circles all across our fields. We'd then go through and chop the heads off with the machete and put them in the middle of the circles in huge piles taking the stalks away to feed to the cattle.

After the barley dried for several more days all the younger women and girls of the village would come together after dark, when the work was done for the day, to work together to remove all the seeds from the tops of the barley stalks. Just the stronger girls and women would do it, as it was hard work that lasted through the whole night until dawn. It was not considered work for the men and boys, only woman's work.

In one given night, there would be four or five groups of girls scattered throughout the fields. Each group, about half a dozen girls, would build a large bonfire so they could see and just have a nice fire going. Then, each girl would get a wooden pole about five feet long and rather thick to pound the barley heads getting all the seeds out. Two girls would work together, filling a round wooden container called a 'moye' made from the trunk of a tree; it looked like a large wooden kettle, actually, but with a very thick bottom. We'd partner up with another girl of similar height, otherwise the pounding would go off balance, then fill our moye about half full with barley. Standing across from each other, we'd pound in unison with our poles, one after the other back and forth, back and forth, back and forth, each taking turns until the barley was all separated from the pod - the secret was a nice steady pace. Imagine the picture, bonfires all across the fields, groups of young women and girls around each fire, pounding with long poles into large wooden bowls, the sounds echoing across the fields. Like something out of an African movie, right?

Once separated, we'd slowly pour the seeds onto a large mat made out of woven grass and, as we poured, the wind would blow through the seeds and separate out the chaffe. If it wasn't a breezy night, we'd try to wait for another night, so we could use the wind rather than having to separate it out by hand.

This was a great time for all of us to get together; many times the boys of the village would come out to the fields and sit around watching us, hoping we would take a break and sit down with them – and sometimes we would unless if older women were there, and they'd yell at us if we'd take a break - then, the boys would run away. The fun part of the night was that we'd make popcorn on the bonfire along with tea and coffee, and take breaks and enjoy the food and the company. We'd bring all the supplies we needed such as pots and cups and glasses and butter for the popcorn.

These nights were very out of the ordinary as the sound of the pounding in wooden drums would be heard all across the fields and could even be heard in the village, fires burning in various places, girls talking, boys coming around and sitting around the fires, and the rest of the village asleep. This would go on all night long until the sun came up in the morning. Many times, the moon would be out so nice and full illuminating the whole field. These were some beautiful nights in the African countryside. It's times like these that I remember so fondly and wish that, for maybe just one night, I could go back and do it again – but just for one night, as it was pretty hard work after a day of grazing the animals and doing farm chores.

By the end of the night, we'd all be so tired, and our hands so blistered and bloody, red and swollen - there was no such thing as gloves – and we'd be all dirty and our eyes itching to death from all the dust and chaffe. Once back home, we'd put goat butter on our hands to soothe them, as goat butter is more delicate and can be used for more versatile things. Finally though, your hands would get calloused and you could do the work more easily. Each year, we'd go through the process of getting our hands destroyed and finally calloused.

Unfortunately, the next day after pounding barley heads all night, we'd have to go on about our chores and do the work that needed to be done - without having any sleep. So, I'd go back home at sunrise, take the donkey down to get water from the river, make some porridge for breakfast, get the animals fed and milked, then take them out to the grasslands to graze. We'd usually skip a night, so we could all rest going back the next night to pound the barley again. This could go on for several weeks or more to finish all the fields for each of the families of the village. It was a nice escape and time to socialize. Now if I could go back for a few days and do it again, it would be great fun. It was hard, but I enjoyed it.

When all was said and done and all the barley pounded and separated, the men would dig a big hole and we'd line it with burlap and pour all the barley seeds into it to save throughout the year until we needed it. We'd keep some at home, but the majority was kept out in these holes in the fields covered with burlap and dirt which we'd open up when we needed some more.

Later in the year, when the next rainy season, Dayr, would arrive in October, we'd start the whole process again with planting, hoeing, chasing the birds away, and harvesting. However, if it didn't rain, we couldn't plant as the fields would be too dry and hard, and we'd just have to get by on what we had stored. Usually, we had enough barley set aside that we could make it through a dry season. But, strangely enough, in spite of the lack of sleep and blistered hands, I always looked forward to the next planting season and all it brought with it. I was recently asked if I'd like to go back and help with the harvest again. My answer? "Sure, but just for one night!"

Chapter Eight

The Nomad's Life

My daughters are approaching their teenage years, and, being the typical American girls, they have their special jewelry and clothes, along with different shades of makeup, cell phones, computers and all the things young girls could want. They also have their girlfriends at school who are just beginning to notice boys. They have their favorite TV programs and are very conscious of their looks. I try to guide them to think about the right things to do in situations, how to be kind to other people, how to respect their elders, all those things that a modern mother and father teach their young daughters. Having studied human development while becoming an RN, it struck me how, at this age, in particular, young adolescents develop a sense of self and their own personal identity, discovering who they are, what they like and don't like, getting in touch with their feelings. I try to help my daughters accept who they are, I praise them all the time, telling them what a good job they're doing, that they're beautiful and intelligent. As their mother, I so appreciate my relationship with them as well as with my young son. We have very open talks about anything, anything they want to talk about. I reassure them, and I don't criticize about anything that would hurt them and their self esteem and personal confidence.

My daughters are learning math and English, science, geography, all the classes that the average girl is learning in school today, and I'm so proud of them. Believe it or not, my daughters, growing up in western culture, are very similar to myself having grown up in Somalia. I remember becoming aware of my looks and trying to make myself look nice, however, the constant criticism that I heard at home from my uncles – you're fat, you're not pretty, your nose is too big, your skin is too dark, you're stupid, wore on me. My self esteem was so low and my confidence so lacking, that I never stood up for myself or tried to make any decisions for my life. I see now that I was so beaten down, that what I did best was simply doing what I was told and never questioning or talking back. I believed that what I had, and what I was doing, was as good as I could have it. My children, now, are so much better equipped to function in life than I was, and I see that it is simply because their self esteem is strong, they like themselves, and they have confidence in themselves and parents that believe in them and encourage them.

Being isolated from society and other people like I was, growing up in our village, made it very difficult for me to be assertive, to tell my grandma and uncles that I didn't want to always be herding the animals, or that I was afraid being out by myself - the only girl amongst all those teenage boys and young men, and that I wanted to be home, back at the village. But, through the years, with no praise for a job well done, or any encouragement to think on my own or make my own decisions, I became little more than a servant girl, rather beaten down, doing whatever I was told to do and doing it quietly without talking back.

When I was ten going on eleven, right about my oldest daughter's age, another dry season hit Somalia; it was a bad one with the grasslands drying up turning totally brown and dusty. My grandma and uncles decided I was old enough to take the sheep and goats way out as a nomad for several months without returning home, just like they did when I had malaria. It was the only way to keep the animals alive for any length of time, and it had to be done or none of us would survive. However, this was usually an older boy's job in the village, as it wasn't safe for a girl to be out by herself as a nomad. In our family, however, I was the boy - or they just didn't care!

I remember that it was getting terribly dry, and we were running out of places to graze the animals, when Grandma said to me, "Habibo, I want you to learn how to take the sheep and goats out by yourself, they need to be brought to where there's rain and grass. We know of a family, related to us, that we want you to go be with them and graze the sheep and goats." My heart sank as I thought to myself, "Oh no, I have to leave home and be out in the wild with people I don't even know?" And, from personal experience, the fear of being beaten up and raped was ever present with me. But, I didn't argue with her and kept my feelings inside, as I got very good at that and doing what I was told. So, my uncle Ahmed arranged for me to take the herd and go along with some distant relatives of ours, a man and his wife and their nephew, Sabriye. They were nomads themselves, spending all their time out wandering the grasslands with no permanent home or village to live in - always pursuing green pastures.

Ahmed knew it rained where they were; however, it was a good three to four day's journey from our village much farther out into the grasslands. So he and I just packed up one day, loaded my essential belongings onto the donkey cart, took all the animals – thirty five sheep and about thirty goats - and started walking. The family we were going to see had no idea we were coming, because there was no way of communication; so, we traveled with all the animals and our belongings in the general direction Ahmed thought they were in.

The land was very parched and dry, and the sheep and goats had very little to eat as we'd walk along. We'd try to walk where we could find water for them, but it wasn't easy, as it hadn't rained for quite some time. We'd sleep each night on the ground with the herd gathered around us for safety as we'd keep an eye out for hyenas trying to get at the herd. And, the next day, we'd just keep on going. Before too long, we got into a part of the country where there were no villages or people, only open grasslands and a few nomads with their herds scattered across the countryside. We'd run across their make-shift huts with a corral made to keep the animals in at night; sometimes we'd come across abandoned ones as the family needed to move on searching for green grass, and sometimes we'd meet with them and get some general ideas as to where our relatives were grazing their herds.

It took us four days of walking to get in the general vicinity of the family we were looking for. As we got closer, several of the nomads we'd meet would give us directions to help us find them. And, as it usually works in Somalia, we eventually located them in a valley, rich with green grass in the shadow of the mountains. They knew Ahmed and welcomed us as their cousins. Ahmed introduced me to them saying, "She'll be staying with you, if that's alright, and she'll be taking care of our herd." The man's name was Mohamed and his son was Sabriye, the woman there was Sabriye's step mother and her name was Hawo. Sabriye, was a few years older than me, perhaps about sixteen, and he became a really good companion to me and, I'd say, we became good friends.

After some greetings and discussion, while I stood there dumbfounded, or like we say in Minnesota, "Like a deer in the headlights," Ahmed simply said good bye to me, and told me to be sure not so lose any of the herd. I can still see him walking away through the grassy field, as I stayed behind with the herd and a family I had never met before. I accepted the situation as something I had to do for the animals to live, and didn't even think about questioning it or speaking my mind. But I can't say I was happy about it. In fact, I was very afraid and on my guard, as I had never been out on my own like this before for weeks and months at a time. And, really, no other ten year old girl had done that before, either. Even the boys, when out as nomads, were at least fourteen or fifteen years old, and they could handle themselves against wild animals and marauders.

Sabriye and I ended up spending all our time grazing our herds together. But his step mother was very unkind, always screaming at us and her husband, very difficult to be around and basically just a very unhappy woman. I tried to avoid her as much as I could. Her husband, the poor man, just kept quiet a lot; I guess because he learned it was safer that way. I learned that same lesson quickly.

For food, Sabriye's mother would only give us milk to eat from the goats, no solid food, so we were always hungry except when we found fruit or some kind of root growing as we walked with the herd. She would make porridge for her and her husband, but not for us. The cow's milk was precious to her, as she'd make butter out of it, so I understand her need as survival is the daily issue out as a nomad. It was easy for us to simply go up to a goat, hold onto one of their back legs, grab a teet and squirt the milk into our mouth. It was gross, however, as thick as half and half with a rather strong taste to it. Most westernized people would find that somewhat distasteful or revolting, however, when you're hungry for days on end, you too would milk the goat and drink its milk. That concept can probably apply to many things. When we're starved for anything, even something distasteful is better than nothing at all. Sabriye, bless his heart, would help, though. Sometimes he would tell me, "Let's switch the goat milk and the cow's milk," which we did at times.

Sabriye's place to sleep was outside the hut, so as to keep an eye on the animals at night, as well as to give his father and step mother their privacy. I would sleep outside the hut as well near the fire, which we'd try to keep going all night long. I remember how it was so cold and lonely at night, laying out there by myself with Sabriye in his little spot, and being with this family I had never met before. If it rained we'd go inside the hut, but I could tell the mother didn't want us in there, so I'd remain very quiet, sitting up against the wall of the hut trying to get some sleep before the sun rose.

My memories of the experience are all mainly sad. I felt like all was just bleak, almost like I had no hope for the future, no control over what I had to do, pushed beyond what I was able to do. It was hard only being able to make friends along the way, and then having to leave them as our lives moved on in different directions.

Sabriye didn't complain too much about it, or his life out as a nomad, since he was used to it, I guess. Also, it was the only life he ever knew. But, now that I look back on it, he was happy to have me out there with him as a friend, someone to talk with and play with rather than being all by himself. I think of him often. He was a very gentle, caring and considerate human being. In fact, I can say I consider him my best friend. He made me feel safe from his step mother as well as the other nomad boys. He took the blame for me when things went wrong, and he stood up for me.

I stayed with this family for three months or so. The step mother simply got more and more hateful as time went on; she would scream at us, even when we hadn't done anything wrong. Sabriye and I just tried to make the best of the situation which, sometimes, that's all you can do. So, when we grazed the animals, we'd try to go where no one ever walked before – virgin territory – so as to hopefully find some fruit or nuts along the way to eat, which we often did. We'd wander many miles just walking and talking, keeping the herd together and all going in the same direction. Sometimes we'd get lost, but would just have to go up onto the mountainside to see where we were and how to find our way back home.

From high up on the mountain sides, we could see many, many miles. We could see everything below us way out, nothing but solid green grass, small lakes scattered across the land catching all the water from the mountains after it rained. We could see paths and trails as well as people with their cows and camels – it was a pretty sight! There were no villages out there in the savannah, just nomads' huts scattered here and there across the land. It was a beautiful part of the country, and it helped to make my loneliness much easier to accept. Plus, my friendship with Sabriye was like a gift from above; I don't see how I would have made it on my own without him to help me and guide me. Life with his mother would have been unbearable! He could have been very mean to me and taken advantage of me, but he didn't, he had a very good soul.

One time, coming down one of the mountainsides, Sabriye was way ahead of me down the mountain leading the herd, while I took up the rear. Working my way through the rocks and down the rough terrain, I lost my footing and fell, tumbling down, down, down a long way, until I finally hit a big rock which stopped my fall. I sprained my ankle really bad and bruised my left hip. I sat there on the mountainside crying for a long time, but Sabriye couldn't hear me from where he was. When he finally realized I wasn't with him, he came back up and helped me scoot down the mountain on my bottom. It was only midday, so we still had to continue herding the animals, even though I was hurt and bruised and cut up.

With swelling setting in after a little while, I couldn't walk; so Sabriye whistled as loud as he could, which is how the nomads communicate to one another. Another young man across the grasslands heard him and came on his camel to help us. Sabriye asked him if he would take me back to the tent, so the boy helped me up onto his camel, which was no easy task as they're very tall, standing about seven feet at the shoulder. I rode on its back, holding onto the hump (only one hump camels in Somalia) all the way back to the tent. I had to hold on really well with not only my hands, but my legs as well; it's a long way down off a camel's back. I spent the rest of the day back at the camp, lying outside, pretty much tending to myself. After sleeping through the night out by the fire, Sabriye and I went out again with the animals, although this time, I had a limp to deal with.

One day, after it had been raining heavily, we were moving the animals across a narrow ravine between two mountains. The ravine was dry when we started to take the animals through, but all of a sudden water started to rush through it. It came so fast and so hard and rose so quickly, that it swept me right off my feet. I tumbled down through the ravine in the rushing water, with it knocking some of the smaller animals down as well. Sabriye grabbed onto me as I was tumbling in the water and helped me up, and then he grabbed onto two small goats that were being washed away also. It was a wild time! Finally, we got out of the rushing water and made it to the side. We were so glad, though, that we didn't lose any of the herd, because if we did lose any animals, we'd be beaten and yelled at. Being all wet and having tumbled down a ravine I could handle, but the wrath of his mother and my grandma and uncles was another story.

I remember a day when we were out in the open land just sitting around playing cards with rocks, while the animals grazed by a river. It was time to move them, so we started walking and headed the two herds to cross a small road. When we were walking, I noticed some blood on the ground, I thought , "Oh my goodness, I'm going to lose a sheep and get into big trouble." I walked along further and found one of my rams all torn up. A "dowaco" as we called it, or jackal, had gotten to him. It must have been hiding in the grass and then jumped out at the animals as they passed by. It ripped the poor ram's underbelly really bad. I panicked and screamed, "I'm going to die, I'm going to die," they're going to kill me. I was so afraid. So, I told Sabriye I was going to take this ram back to the tent while he watched the herd. I tied a rope to the ram's neck and pulled him back to the tent. When I got there, I was crying and told his mother I didn't know what happened, and that I was so sorry. She told me, "Don't ever let it happen again. This time you're forgiven, but if it ever happens again, you're going to be in serious trouble and be beaten severely."

The ram was going to die, so all we could do was slaughter it and eat it. In the bush, there is no way to preserve or keep food for any length of time, so, when an animal was slaughtered, that's what we ate until the whole thing was gone. The tradition is to fry the liver and kidneys, which were delicacies, and they're eaten by the elders - Sabriye's parents in this case; the stomach and head were made into soup; the rest of the meat was cut into small pieces and laid in the sun to dry, then fried with the fat. Nothing was wasted. So for two weeks we feasted, until all was completely gone. However, I was still worried what my grandmother and uncles would have to say.

Life went on this way for several months. We moved the hut often as the animals grazed out the grass around us. I got used to being with this family and just tried to avoid the step mother and take care of my own business herding the animals. She, in turn, pretty much left me alone. Goat's milk wasn't that great to drink all the time, but at least I had that to keep me from starving, and I'd find little things to eat while out grazing.

Finally, my Grandma and Ahmed came to get me. I really had no idea when they'd be coming, but I did know that eventually they would. Towards evening one day, they just showed up walking across the open land. I was so glad to see them, realizing that my time out there was finished, and I could go back home. It had been very hard work sleeping on the ground every night, getting yelled at by the step mother, and having very little to eat. But, I made it. I learned that, as humans, we can endure a lot – sometimes very difficult times, and, as long as we don't give up and keep hoping, life changes as it does and things get better. My grandma and Ahmed weren't very demonstrative, but they told me I did a good job, and it was time to come home now, as the rains had returned to our village. So, we slept by the fire that night, and in the morning, gathered the herd together and started our walk back to the village where life would resume its normal routine. I never appreciated "the normal routine" so much as when my time out with Sabriye and his family was over.

Chapter Nine

The Dark Before the Dawn

Another very dry season came to Somalia about a year or so after I had been out with Sabriye and his family. Everything dried up, the grass became brown, leaves withered up and fell of all the bushes, there was dust was everywhere. All the villagers were running out of areas to graze their animals, and we were using up all our stored corn, barley stalks and hay; cows eat so much more than sheep and goats, it was almost impossible to keep them fed during a dry season. Finally, the situation became desperate, and my grandmother and uncles decided it would be best to move the cows, fifty five in all, far out into the grasslands where the grass wasn't green, it was brown and dry, but there was plenty of it.

I was about twelve years old at this time, and my heart started sinking when I heard the talk about having to take the cows out and graze them. I just knew I'd be the one to take them. Memories of my last time, even though I enjoyed having Sabriye as a friend, came flooding back: the loneliness, being afraid and hungry, and the difficult lifestyle as a nomad. Sure enough, my grandmother told me that I'd have to go and take the cows. She and Ahmed were going to stay home and care for the sheep and goats, but they knew of a family that was grazing their animals way out in the grasslands, where I could take the cows. Little did I know that my last time out as a nomad was a beautiful experience compared to what I was in for.

I had no choice in the matter; I didn't even voice my opinion as to why Ahmed couldn't come along or even my grandmother. By this time in my life, I just did what I was told. My spirit was broken. I was like a slave. This time of my life was by far the lowest point in my life. I felt as though the cows were more important than me, which I knew was true. I felt no one cared whether I lived or died, was raped or murdered; as long as the cows were being fed, it didn't matter how I felt or what I wanted. No one ever asked me what I wanted or what I needed - or, for starts, if I actually wanted to go! Imagine a child working sixteen hours per day, seven days per week, three hundred and sixty five days per year. No rest, no winter or spring break, no one saying "You're tired today. Let me take the cows out and you rest." I have to say, I never said the word, "No" until I was seventeen years old.

Without even a protest from me, my uncle, Ahmed, and I packed up my meager belongings, which I carried on my back, and early one morning took all the cows and calves and started walking. We walked all day long through dry and dusty land: no grass, the bushes nothing but skeletons, and no water anywhere. We camped that night around a fire, got up the next day, milked some of the cows so we'd have something for breakfast, and walked another whole day again.

Walking with Ahmed, I fell into a deep despair. I didn't share any of my feelings with him. I couldn't. I didn't have it in me. I had plenty of time to think, though. I remember feeling that I didn't care anymore if I lived or died. I was a beaten down spirit, desperate to get out of that living situation. The only way I made it through life at this point, was to continue praying, "Help me, God! Is this all there is for me." The only option for me was to hope for marriage and continue the same lifestyle. I had very bad feelings about my mother and father, anyone that had the power to come to help me, but didn't. I thought about the other village girls who were so much better off than me. They had parents, didn't have to be a nomad by themselves, didn't do farm chores, and certainly weren't out walking behind a herd of cattle through the barren land. I wasn't like the other girls.

Finally, through word of mouth from nomads we met along the way, we found the hut of the family we were looking for around 8:00 pm on the second night. It was just a mother and her three teenage sons at home for the night sitting around a fire. The sons were a few years older than me; their father had died several years earlier. They were true nomads, constantly having to move their animals from one rainy season to the next all throughout Somalia, going to town only once in a great while to sell their animals and buy a few supplies. Ahmed spoke with the mother and introduced me, asking if I could stay by them and take our cattle out. He assured her I would find my own places so as not to interfere with their herds of cattle, camels, sheep and goats. She agreed. However, I could see the three boys having some mischief in their eyes, when they saw that a twelve year old girl would be joining them all by herself. By this time in my life, I came to recognize that look, and I learned to always be on my guard. My heart sank as I, once again, knew I'd be fighting to keep from being molested. I knew I'd be with them for several months.

None of them greeted me with warmth. They were somewhat odd - nice, but not cheerful. I imagine being out by themselves their whole lives made them somewhat different than village people. The oldest son, Hassan, welcomed me. He was kind and some-what nice, seeming like he took the place of his father.

The first night we got there, we were tired, exhausted, our feet were sore and burning, and we were hungry. We again milked some of the cows for our supper. He and I settled the cattle down for the night, as well as ourselves, sand slept outside the hut, right on the ground, side by side near the fire. I had one wrap to cover myself with, and that's what I used as my blanket the whole time I was there. My bed remained a little spot outside the hut, where I made a bed of grass and leaves.

When Ahmed left early the next morning, before sunrise, all he said was, "Take care of yourself." And off he went walking away, and there I was with. All I wanted to do was cry, which I held in until I was by myself.

Well, it was what it was, nothing I could do about it. So, that morning, the three boys and I took all the animals far from their tent to graze in the grasslands. It was a pretty impressive herd – very large! We left early that morning, as I then did each morning thereafter. It was barely bright enough to see. We walked for two hours or so, the animals grazing as they could. They all mixed together, and the four of us, one in front, the rest of us on the sides and the rear, just kept them going, each one of us having our long shepherd's stick. The animals stuck together, as they're pretty smart that way, knowing it would be death for them to wander off by themselves. I remember it being so very dry - dry grass everywhere coming way up above your knees. They showed me an area for my cows to graze and taught me a few whistles to make as a signal between us if I got lost, and they warned me not to wander off too far. So, this first time, I was pretty cautious and stayed fairly close to what looked familiar to me, while they went off in different directions.

I spent that day afraid. I didn't know who all was in the area; I didn't know what kind of animals I'd encounter; I did know, however, that there would be no other girls to be friends with. I felt I had no hope. I thought, why me? I was sad. That's when I was able to cry.

I was nervous that morning. These nomad guys were known to be dangerous, very rough and aggressive, living out in the bush all the time. Rumor had it

that the camel's milk, which they drank, was an aph-
rodisiac which made them even more aggressive. I was
so worried I'd get raped or lose my cows. I didn't know
which would be worse, probably losing the cows - or
even one cow!

The second day I was there, I went with Hassan to
the one watering spot, where everyone took their herds
for water. We walked and walked, at least half the day,
leaving before sunrise with about one hundred and
fifty cows between us. All we had to eat that morning
was milk, which wasn't very filling. In fact, that's what I
had to eat every day and nothing else except what dried
fruit and nuts I could find. I got used to being hungry,
and I got very used to living off nothing but milk.

We got to the well about high noon and had to wait
our turn, as others were there before us. This was the
central gathering spot for everyone. Each day, there
would be several nomads there with their herds at any
given time. It was a busy place: cows bellowing, bells
on the lead cows ringing, nomad boys and men yelling, dust filling the air. When we arrived, there were
lots of people there, forty or so. There was even a little
makeshift café to buy tea and bread.

When it was our turn, Hassan showed me how to
draw the water out of the well with a bucket tied to a
rope. We'd then pour it into a big tank and let the cows,
four or five at a time, drink to their fill. Of course, the
law of nature governed as the stronger cows got the
water first, pushing their way in to the trough, then
finally the weaker ones would get their drinks also.
That law of nature held true for the nomads as well.

It took us about an hour or so to water all of the cows. Then, came the best part. We pulled the buckets up for ourselves, poured it over our heads and bodies, clothes and all, and washed all the dust and dirt off. I wasn't wearing any head covering at this time, because I wasn't married, so I'd just wash my hair with water, no soap of course – no such thing for nomads. Hassan was nice to me, and I liked him; we both cleaned up and cooled off, then started heading back towards home, as it would take the better part of the afternoon to get back to the hut.

After that first time, I took my herd of cows to the well by myself. Many times there were others there before me, so I'd have to wait my turn. Sometimes they were nice and would let me go ahead of them, or they'd help me lift the water out of the well and pour it into the trough. Other times, they'd take advantage of me, pushing me and my herd out of the way, harassing me and calling me names, or just basically trying to intimidate me. Each time I went there, I'd hope there wouldn't be rough people around the well, as this was also my time to cool off and wash all the dust and dirt off myself and my clothes. But, if there was trouble around, I'd just water the cows and leave as soon as I could.

Each day, I'd leave before sunrise and take the herd out by myself. Oddly enough, the cows knew where to go, so I'd just follow along with my stick making sure they stayed together, until we found some grass patches for them to eat on. Sometimes, I'd run into other nomads. Most were teenagers a little older than me, and they'd ask me where I was from. So, we'd visit a little and talk about home. They'd tell me where they had been, and if I thought they were safe, we'd visit for a while. Some talked about rumors war which was ramping up pretty good in the country, especially in the larger cities. Up until this time, I had no idea that war was brewing in the country. I didn't realize how that civil war would change my life; that it was actually an answer to my prayers.

While out by myself, if I saw camel boys and their herds, I'd hide myself in the bushes or trees or in some ditch, so they wouldn't see me. I spent much of my time like this, hiding in the woods being afraid. I avoided them at all costs, they were older and stronger and very aggressive. Anytime I heard someone coming with their herd, I'd climb a tree or some tall bush to see if I knew them. It always made me nervous. If there were several of them, they'd be much more bold. Many times I'd have to hide in the trees, so they wouldn't find me; otherwise, there was nothing I could do. They'd come my way and ask me if I was there by myself. I always made up a story that someone was around, like my uncle or brothers; that they were just over the hillside and would hurt them if they touched me.

It was probably living in the wild like they were that allowed for their aggression. They had very little contact with the outside world, no education, and no law anywhere to lay down anything like right and wrong. It was just the law of nature. If there was only one of them trying to get me, I would fight and sometimes win. I always had my stick with me, and I'd put up a good fight. I'd hit them with it right in their crotch. But, if there was more than one or a group, which happened quite often, I wouldn't fight. What was going to happen was inevitable. I was just thankful that I hadn't reached maturity yet and couldn't get pregnant. Sadly, I had to be on the alert every day, all day, ready to fight at any moment. It was hard to sit, watch the cows and relax, because at any moment, I could be attacked. To this day, I have to admit, I'm on alert. Not that I'm afraid of being molested, but my inner being is just on alert. It's hard for me to relax, but I'm working on it.

Each night, back at the camp, we'd keep the fire going all night long to ward off the wild animals, so it was nice and warm to lay there by the fire. The three boys and I slept outside, while their mother slept inside the hut. I guess she wasn't concerned with me being out there with her sons, because I could have slept in the hut with her. However, sometimes it was so hot that she'd sleep out there with us. The animals were in their makeshift corrals, but they could still be attacked, especially the young ones. We could hear the wild animals out in the grasslands and forests howling and growling, hyenas, jackals and sometimes a lion even though they were getting scarce. As long as we kept a fire going and stayed close to it with the herd, we were all safe.

I remember being so very afraid sleeping outside with not only the wild animals, but the three teenage boys as well. I knew from experience that this was a dangerous situation. It wasn't often, I'm sure, that they had a twelve year old girl sleeping outside with them by the fire, while their mother slept soundly inside the tent. So, when I slept, I wrapped my little shawl around me, laid on the ground and tied my legs together with a rope, that I had woven together out of long grass. That way, they would not be able to rape me as easily. I slept this way all the time that I was there, because I could not trust the boys due to my previous experiences. Have you ever tried to sleep with a rope tied around your legs? Probably not, but maybe you could try it sometime – for the whole night!

Most of the time, my days were spent sitting in the sunshine, making ropes or pretend dolls out of sticks and grass or trying to find dry fruits. Sometimes, I'd just sit there and cry. I felt out of place, tired, always hungry, dirty, and I knew I had lice but couldn't get rid of them – no comb to get them out. I'd sing whatever songs I could remember, thinking that perhaps it was soothing to the cows. I'd think about my life a lot, really having no one that cared for me. I thought about getting married and having children of my own someday. I kept thinking there had to be more in the world for me; I hated my situation, now stuck out in the grasslands with nothing but hyenas and jackals and boys older than me, always leering at me and trying to get me down on the ground for their own pleasure. I lived like this for several months, never really knowing when I'd be going home. I kept hearing that it didn't rain back home, so I knew it could be a long time. However, the cows were doing well and grandma was happy.

To make matters worse, there would be weird people going from hut to hut at night to steal or rape - night stealers or night rapers, we'd call them. One night, several weeks after I got there, we heard yelling and crying and screaming coming from another family's tent not too far in the distance from ours. Hassan said, "Stay here, I'll check it out." So he ran to the tent where the screams were coming from. It was a mother with her two daughters and son that lived there. There was a big strong guy who got into the hut trying to take some sugar and food from them, then, on his way out he tried to rape the woman. She kicked him, and as he was trying to get away, she grabbed his ankle and wouldn't let him go. He kicked and punched, dragging her fifty feet or more away from her hut, as she refused to let him go. By this time several other guys from other tents in the area ran to her, got the guy and tied him to a tree. When the sun came out the next morning, we all came to check him out. The men tried to teach him a lesson; they beat him up pretty badly and told him to leave that area and not do that again. Hopefully, he heeded their warning.

During my nomadic life there, I became very thin with tape worms and lost a lot of weight, not to mention the head lice. You could tell just by looking at me, that I was not very happy. I was very tired, worn out, tired of being afraid and fighting and being abused, and I was very lonely. To me, this was the very darkest part of my life. To the point of despair, I almost gave up – sad for a twelve year old girl! But, always to remember, the dawn comes after the darkest part of the night, not before.

As time went on, I became more of a loner with this family, and that's how I survived, just sticking to myself, keeping my nose clean, not needing any help from anyone, and putting on a tough exterior. The boys didn't really talk to me, or have much to do with me; being scared and nervous, I didn't really welcome any friendship from them. Plus, I think the feeling of being alone, being helpless to do anything about it, and being in such a fearful situation caused me to become very withdrawn.

Being out as a nomad like this, however, had its payoff for me in the long run. It was hard and scary and lonely, but from it I learned how to be strong and assertive, able to depend on myself, always on my guard, never trusting anyone in order to survive. I still have trouble knowing how to be comfortable and relax, so I guess in a way, I'm still a nomad protecting myself. I learned to be very stoic and not emotional, basically thinking, "This is what you have to do now, you have no choice, so just do it." That attitude has helped me as I came to America. Believe me, starting up a life in America and becoming successful is not easy, but I did it!

One day, completely unexpected, one of my uncles, Abdi, came to see how I was doing. I was very surprised to see him, as he rarely left the farm. I was so glad to see him, even if he was always criticizing and making fun of me. I welcomed him, thinking maybe my time out there was over, and I'd be going back to the village. However, after seeing that the cows were in good shape, he just said that he'd see me later, and he left, turning around and walking back to the village. He didn't even take notice of how I was.

My spirit was close to being broken. I now know how a prisoner feels locked up in a terrible place with no hope of getting out, and having to fight for his or her life every single day. I see where people just give up and let life do to them what it will. I felt so discouraged, I needed to go home so badly; I felt like my life had turned into a nightmare.

Life went on, day after day, the same story. Two months later, my other uncle, Ahmed came to see me. He took one look at me, not at the cows, and said, "I do not like what I see, Habibo. We're going back to the village, the cows can eat corn stalks. You're so thin and you have lice." I was so happy! Ahmed was always my saviour, the only one that cared for me. Really, he was the father I never had. Oddly enough, I had mixed feelings about going back to the life I had in the village. It wasn't a whole lot better, but I had to go.

To this day, I question how they could have done that to a young girl, how they could possibly not have not known what would happen to me. I question how that was acceptable to anyone: my mother, my father who knew where I was, my grandma and uncles. I still ask myself this question, "How was that acceptable?" Why wasn't there anyone there for me to say, "Get this girl out of here; get her into school; give her some decent clothes." I see, but wish I didn't have to accept, that the cows were more important than I was. For so long, I had hoped that perhaps there were some feelings for me, but, unfortunately that wasn't the case. A friend of mine said to me when I was questioning how that was acceptable, "Habibo, it wasn't acceptable. It's as simple as that. It just wasn't acceptable." That's a hard thing to take, but it happens to us. We're not always promised people around us that care for us; sometimes we have just the opposite. But it's important, very important, to care for ourselves and not give up on hope.

Ahmed and I took the cows and walked one whole day towards the village, only getting about half way there. We camped that night, making a fire, and sleeping around it. I was happy to be taken out of the grasslands with all those boys and having to fend for myself. We slept that night around the fire, then the next day, milked the cows for our breakfast, and walked another entire day and evening.

Finally, we arrived at the village around 9:00, completely tired and exhausted, barely able to walk anymore and covered in dust and dirt and lice. I remember being so happy to hear the sounds of the village and see the smoke rising from the fires at the people's huts. When I came into my grandmother's hero and into her hut, she did not even get up to greet me. Instead she said, "Aren't you going to come over here and give me a hug?" I felt bad about that, like I wasn't loved; that I was just a farm hand. Putting the cows in their corral, I ate what supper there was left and fell onto my bed and slept.

The very next morning, before the sun came up, my grandmother woke me up, "Habibo, Habibo, wake up, time to get up and get chores done. You have to take the cows out today. I couldn't believe it; I was expected to get up and do the usual chores of making a fire, getting water at the river, getting breakfast ready for everyone, and then afterwards, take the cows out to graze. I got up, got water from river, took the cows out, and did what I had to do.

Before I left that day with the herd, my grandmother did what she thought was best to get rid of my lice. With a razor, she shaved all the hair off my head down to my scalp and rubbed laundry detergent flakes into my scalp. And, this is how I went out that day, being told, leave this on for a while, then rinse it off in the river. Later that day, I rinsed it off, but got a terrible headache from the detergent. It was the worst headache I've ever had. It stayed with me the rest of the day and all night. I couldn't close my eyes, and felt like my head was about to burst. I sat up all night by myself in the dark, outside the hut.

The next morning, I was expected to take the cows out. With my head shaved like a man, the other young people of the village laughed at me and called me names, telling me I was like a boy and making fun of me. I was so crushed. I thought to myself, I will never get married. No one in their right mind would ever love me. I look so hideous. Slowly, however, my hair grew back, very slowly!

Oddly enough, I felt stronger that I survived the nomad experience out by myself. I was soon the talk of the village. "Habibo took her grandma's cows out by herself." "Habibo took the cows way out in the country for a long time." "Ooh, she is strong." "She does anything she's asked to do." "She will make good wife." I was praised for it. I proved myself.

I began to see clearly that my life with my grandmother was temporary. My mind was made up, that I was going to leave. I thought, if I do it for a few more years, that's OK. But, it will be over soon. So, I did what I could to look nice and continued on.

Later that year, because the dry seasons continued to be very harsh, we had to move again to graze the animals. This time it wasn't so bad, as my grandmother and Ahmed came along. Perhaps Ahmed had something to do with that, after he saw what happened to me when I was out alone.

We walked the animals all the way to the border of Ethiopia and stayed for several months camping from site to site. We brought barley, butter, milk, and tea and camped close to the river, so we could get water for us and for the animals. Ahmed always slept outside, but Grandma and I slept in the hut. While we were out this time, I took the goats and sheep, Ahmed took the cows, and Grandma stayed behind with the younger calves, sheep and goats. This was one of the better memories of living with my grandmother, I think my grandmother realized that I was becoming a woman and whether she liked or not she would lose me soon enough. I think though deep down grandmother did not want a village life for me. I also think that is why she used to kick out the boys when they come to our hut to talk to me. It was almost like a vacation being a way from uncle Abdi and meeting news friends and people was really fantastic.

I look back on it now, and I think things had changed between us after my experience taking the cows out by myself. I was older now, ready for marriage, and I was much stronger and sure footed than I was before. The nomadic experience, out by myself and fighting for my life, gave me a confidence I never had before. It clarified, in my mind, what I wanted out of life – and it wasn't life as I knew it!

I made a decision that I didn't want to live in my grandma's house anymore, and I would spend much of my time, as the goats were grazing, thinking about how I would get away. I thought the only way to get out of my situation, was to get married and live with a husband, maybe having a hut and a few animals of my own. While we were out, a boy named Zak, who was out with his family grazing their animals as well, liked me. He would come to our tent at night while my grandma and I were sleeping, he would try to wake me up, but grandma had four eyes as she seem to wake up the instance she hear noise. She kicked him out and told him never to come back again. She also told me if she ever sees me talking to him, my behind would show for it, in other words get ready to be whipped. For some reason or another, my grandmother did not like this boy. I think it was more likely that she didn't like his tribe which was different than ours. She usually did not mind when boys came by the hut to talk to me, but this time she became really furious with me. She demanded that I not talk to him any longer, and if I did, the consequences would be terrible.

So, Zak and I made plans to run away together and get married. We set up an appointed one night, when we would leave; he was to come by our tent around midnight. I was up and ready, while my grandmother slept. I slipped outside the hut and waited. Well, he never came! I was sad and very disappointed. However, I did get to the point in my mind of deciding to leave, and I almost did it. It was probably a blessing, though, that I did not get married at such a young age and under those circumstances. I, most likely, would be out grazing animals right now, or at the least, taking care of my children in my hut.

This also is where I had my first marriage offer. I was thirteen, and an eighteen year old wanted to marry me. The question came from his father to my grandma. He came to our hut and said, "Oh, your granddaughter, Habiba, is so well behaved and works so hard. I never see her complain, even at night when she's with the cows. She's always working. I'd like my son to marry her."

My Grandma said, "No, Habibo is not ready for marriage." But I really think she and my uncles weren't ready to let me go, as they wanted me to help with the work. Then the father proposed to my grandmother, saying, "Well, then, how about if I marry you?" My grandmother was in her late 50's and told him, "No."

There was another older woman who would graze her cows near us also, and I spent much of my time with her out in the grasslands. She was deformed, the poor thing, and not suitable to be married. She had physical abnormalities and that was not handled very well in our culture. So, she stayed single. We would play around the cows, and boys grazing their animals would come around to play with us and talk, but never threatened to hurt us because of the older woman being there. I got to like her a lot. Knowing her and spending time together, made that trip out to the grasslands an even nicer experience.

I was very glad to be away from our home place in the village where my uncle, Abdi and his wife stayed behind to watch the place. His constant criticism is what hurt most – the emotional abuse. He used to say that no one would ever marry me, that my skin was too dark or my nose too big. He would say, "Your mom should have done something with your nose when you were born. I think that is why your dad divorced your mother." He had lots of health problems, and I think some of his bitterness came from that. It seems that he was always unhappy and bitter, very frustrated, and this was his way of dealing with his anger over his illness. At times he could be nicer, and at other times he was angry at the entire world. Abdi is at peace now, having died several years ago from his struggles with untreated tuberculosis.

Chapter Ten

War

Civil War took hold of Somalia as early as 1980, right before I was born. Prior to this, the leader of the country, General Barre and his Supreme Revolutionary Council took on the philosophy of scientific socialism, because they were aligning themselves with the Soviet Union for assistance against Ethiopia. General Barre used his military force and terror to take the farmlands from the people, giving then to his own tribes; this caused much anger amongst the people, especially because their land was given to opposing tribes. Unfortunately, the winds of friendship sometimes are fickle, and the Soviet Union, in the late seventies, aligned itself with Ethiopia and supplied many troops and aid to them, so they could defeat Somalia in the fight over the area called the Punta land. Because of that, General Barre cut off his friendship with the Soviet Union and became friends with the United States, who then supplied Somalia with aid and troops and war machines. The fighting continued, and

General Barre continued favoring his tribe and clans over others, and before we knew it, civil war broke out. I was not aware of the fighting or the trouble the country was in until it started to reach our village.

Living in Balcad as I did, sheltered me from much of what was happening in the rest of the country, as we were many miles from any of the larger cities like Mogadishu on the Indian Ocean, or Berbere on the Gulf of Aden. Looking back, I think perhaps my mother, or God had me stay there, as she knew I would be safer with the cows, goats, sheep, a few crocodiles, and hyenas, than I would be with her in Mogadishu.

In 1991, General Barre was ousted from power by the very tribes he took land from, and he escaped from the capital of Mogadishu. He was of the Darod tribe, and he and his tribe were ousted by the Haweye tribe which is the large parent tribe of mine. Anyone in the country of the Darod tribe and lineage was in great danger of being killed and many were, such as my mother's second husband who also fled from Mogadishu.

I remember a lot of chaos and a lot of people moving in many directions, with a sense of loss that I had never seen before coming over us in the village. Even though I was young and did not understand the seriousness of the situation we were in and what the war brought upon us, I could sense that things would never be the same for many of us.

Each day, we started to hear reports that in Mogadishu some of the neighbor's relatives died in a bombing, or someone's whole family was executed, or their house was bombed and everyone blown up with it. Every day some new tragedy happened and people were killed. All the land that General Barre took over under the Soviet Union's scientific socialism and distributed to those tribes that were close to him, was taken back by the original tribal members; the men, women and children living on the land were annihilated. The fierceness of tribalism returned to the country, and it became tribe against tribe, clan against clan, all over Somalia. I heard that some women and children – boys and girls - of a certain tribe to the west of us were walking, no husbands with them, and they were all raped and killed.

Soon, before we knew it, our whole village was full of new comers from the cities. Some were relatives that we had never seen before; some were pure strangers fleeing for their lives across the country - all seeking safety. The sad part was that if the people were of a different parent tribe or sub-tribe than our village, then they had to keep on going as they weren't welcome. I'm not sure where they went, probably Kenya.

At one point, there were four or five other families living with us in the village, all having put up their huts next to ours and within our fences trying to stay alive. We used a lot of our supplies to try to feed them, and we even ran out of barley which we grew a lot of. Oddly enough, I didn't interact with them much because they didn't mix with country people, as we were considered rough and crude and uneducated. I guess we were all of those things, but we were happy to let them put up their huts, share our food and try to help them. Plus, I was shy then and stayed to myself most of the time.

My grandmother would try to shield me from many things about the war, but I could still feel that the country was heading for the worse. As time went on, our entire village ran out of many supplies. In the past, we went to Beledwayne to sell our livestock in exchange for goods, but Beledwayne fell to a different tribe, and all the people living there were either killed or had to leave the city with nothing as the other tribe now took control – and only about thirty miles from Balcad. So, we had nowhere to go or anyone to sell the goats or sheep to, as it became very dangerous to travel anywhere, and supplies became unaffordable. So we had no money or necessary supplies - no sugar, no oil, no clothing, no rice, no tea - nothing. Milk became the main food source for most people who had cows or goats. If we could, perhaps we would trade for some tea or some other item within the village or from the people seeking refuge with us. Many of those that came to the village, unfortunately, decided to return to the cities as they couldn't get used to the hard life. They tried to fit in and help with chores, but it would have taken them years to get used to that. I feared for them as they headed back to the large cities and I really don't think they made it very long.

One day, to our complete surprise, my mother just walked into the village without any forewarning. She came all the way from Mogadishu, much of the way on foot. She looked pretty rough - so tired and very pregnant, probably seven to eight months along at the time. She was so exhausted, and you could see she had worry in her eyes. She told us she was robbed of everything she had in her apartment and had to flee the city as her husband went the other direction out of Somalia, running for his life being of the Darod tribe.

I hadn't seen her for several years, so I was ecstatic to see her and thought she was going to stay with us forever. When mother visited us in the past, she always brought me things - dresses, jewelry, little things, but this time was different; all she had was the dress she was wearing, dirty and worn as it was, nothing else. I guess you could say, "How do you expect your mother to bring you something when there is war going on? Hah!" But you have to understand that sometimes children have expectations and think that their parents are untouchable and can pull some kind of magic together to get things done. I asked her, "Did you bring something for me, Hoyo (mama)?" She said "No, Habiba, I had no time to prepare; I had to leave very quickly and at night. I promise to bring you something the next time I come back."

My mother told us she was going to stay with us for awhile, and that she would be going back to have her baby in Mogadishu and then on to Kenya where she hoped to meet up with her husband. She left after a few weeks, even though things did not improve at all in the country; she knew it wasn't safe, but she was going to go anyway. Years later, I asked my mother why she left the village since there was nothing in Mogadishu for her. She said that our family was very poor, and had nothing to help her with, so her best chance was to emigrate and go out of Somalia after she had the baby. We didn't hear from her for quite some time, and then we got a letter stating she had a baby girl named Naima, and that she was leaving for Nairobi, Kenya the next month. Little did I know that several years later, I'd be joining her myself as we made our way to Dadaab.

My youngest uncle, Ali, was also missing at that time in Mogadishu. No one knew where he was or heard anything from him either. My grandmother was worried a lot about him, and the fact he was her baby, made it even harder. She would ask anyone who arrived in our village if they have seen him, but no news came of him. Ali had luck with him though, and after about a year he came home having lived in empty houses in Mogadishu and having only one meal if it was a good day. When he came to the village he was so thin, he looked ragged and worn out with his hair all shaved like he came from prison. We were glad to have him home. I forgave him for what he did to me as a little girl, and our relationship improved. He slept outside with Ahmed on the same filiq (rug) and helped with chores; he's been there ever since. He married after I left the country and had children, unfortunately, three of whom died from malaria.

Ever since 1991, things haven't really gotten any better in Somalia. In fact, it got ten times worse than what I remember. It is so really bad, very bad: no government, everyone on their own, many tribes controlling various areas, many breakouts and fights and people getting killed for no reason. The poverty level is extremely high with no jobs, hunger, younger kids suffering, no way of getting aid and supplies to the country. Whenever I call back home and talk to a relative there's always news of how someone died or someone got killed or someone got raped and robbed.

About six months ago, I got a voice mail from a younger cousin saying that my uncle's son was riding a bike when he and about twenty two other people were killed by a bomb. It's very sad and discouraging for me to hear that, but I am lucky that I and my children are safe here in America and away from all that. But think of how you would feel if you had to flee from your own country which you grew up in and loved and could never go back. It's sad that many parts of Africa and the world are like that. Unfortunately, the people aren't willing to put their greediness and hunger for power aside for the sake of the country.

Around 1992, the people in my village started to hear rumors of the front lines of fighting getting closer and closer to our village, breaking out here and there in different parts of the neighboring villages with the various tribes trying to take each other over. Our tribe, the Hawaadle tribe, was fighting with our neighboring tribe called the Habargidir tribe. Our men and boys would go out and fight with them at night, trying to keep them from taking over our village. They'd go out at night so as to hide and not be seen so easily; then they would pull back and return to the village during the daytime. Many were stationed out at a distance and stayed there all the time trying to hold the Habargidir back.

We girls and women were very afraid, because at times the opposing tribes would enter the villages and kill and rape and steal; the females in any village were not safe, from little girls to older women, sometimes even boys. I knew some girls that were raped, and I heard it while it was happening – screaming, fighting, crying – it was a horrible sound filled with anguish. So, each night all of us females would gather up a few belongings and small blankets from our huts, and go to the woods to spend the night - hiding amongst the trees, leaving our animals back at our huts inside their fences. Our half of the village would hide on the east side past the river, and the other half would hide on the west side. We'd sleep on the floor of the jungle with our blankets over us, all huddled together. Then, each morning, we'd return to the village and do our work taking care of the animals, cooking, and milking the cows and goats. We'd also take care of the wounded and dead soldiers and then prepare for the next night in the woods.

This was the first time in my life that I saw death and terrible suffering. Each day, as the men and boys would return to the village from fighting, we'd hear of who died or got hurt the night before. I knew many of them that were killed; it was a horrible time. One time, a missile went off right over my head, so close that I could feel the heat of it, as it passed by my hair.

Each day, however, after sleeping in the forest at night with the other women and girls, I continued to take our animals out to graze as they needed to eat even if there was trouble in the area. When I'd be out with them, I could hear the sounds of war – guns blasting off in the distance, bazookas firing, and women and girls getting raped not very far from me. Unfortunately, the sound of that was common in Somalia even before the war, and we were all used to hearing it. I was taught just to turn the other way and move on, which everyone did.

This kind of life, in the middle of tribes fighting one another, bombs going off and guns shooting, sounds of rape, and no supplies went on for about a year with many, many men and boys fighting, while the women and girls, each night, would hide in the woods for fear of getting raped. Eventually, however, foreign solders came into the village and surrounding area - American soldiers went to Mogadishu; in our village, we had the Canadian soldiers. They liked us little kids, and every day would give us cookies and treats. Many times I'd ask if I could ride on top of their army tank, and they'd lift me up and let me sit on top as it drove around.

In 1993, eighteen U.S. soldiers were killed in Mogadishu in an effort to capture General Mohamed Farrah Aidid who was in control at the time. This became famous through the movie, Black Hawk Down. It was a very unfortunate incident, but the Somali forces were fierce and fighting for their lives. Unfortunately, on March 31, 1994, all the U.S. and Canadian soldiers left Somalia, when President Clinton pulled the troops out of the country, because the people in America didn't want their troops there.

It was very hard seeing war come to our country. Life before had been difficult at best with plenty of hard work, but there was a peacefulness about it, as we all went about our routine of doing our daily chores, taking care of the animals, and going out to the fields. Our world was much smaller before the war came. It extended from our village to about a hundred or more miles in every direction. Once war came, our world got much larger, as people from all over came through the village. Even the soldiers from other countries were a reminder that the world was much bigger than we realized. I had never heard of Canada or some of the other countries we came in contact with. Now, all of a sudden, I was riding on army tanks with soldiers - white ones at that!

Chapter Eleven

Answered Prayers

———•─••─•———

It was the Fall of 1995, after several rounds of nomadic life and the fighting amongst the tribes getting worse and worse, that my grandmother received a letter from my mother begging that she and my uncles let me come to help her with her four children in Nairobi, Kenya. She was there due to her second husband having to flee the country for his safety, and, as is the case many times in Somalia, he was now living with a different woman. The letter was given to a man who had come from Nairobi who then gave it to one of the local farmers who was selling his herd in Beledwayne. He, then, delivered it to us in the village.

I wasn't aware that a letter had been received and that my leaving was being discussed. I did know, however, that I was getting to the age where I could be married soon, as thirteen or fourteen is prime time for a Somali girl to be married, and I knew this would be my ticket out. Several of the boys from the village were, in a sense, courting me as we'd get together and talk, spend time together, seeing if we liked each other. My grandmother and uncles realized they were probably going to lose me before too long, as once I got married, I'd be moving in with my husband on his father's farm and helping there.

My grandmother, one day, said to me, "Habibo, your mother would like you to go to Nairobi with her and help her. We are considering letting you go, but haven't decided just yet." I got all excited at the thought that perhaps I'd be able to leave there and all the work I was required to do with little or no thanks. I prayed and prayed that they would allow me to leave and that my life would change; just the thought of being with my mother and four siblings, to me, would be like going to paradise, even if it was in a poor section of Nairobi with little or no money. Anything, to me, seemed better than the continued hard labor I had to do. I overheard the discussions that were going on regarding my leaving; my uncle, Ahmed, was OK with me going, and, after awhile, my other uncle, Abdi came around and agreed that they would lose me anyway so they might as well let me go. I was ecstatic hearing that kind of talk! Finally, after a few days, my grandmother told me they decided it would be alright to let me go and be with my mother and four siblings who I had never met. I was beside myself! Finally, I would be leaving!

It was very hard for me to imagine a life outside the village, where herding animals, working in the fields and going out as a nomad was all I knew. My living situation and the work put on me, I did not like and hoped and prayed, with all my heart, would somehow change. But I didn't know much about the outside world except for the few weeks I spent with my mother in Mogadishu when I had malaria. I did like what I saw, however. I knew Nairobi was a very large city with cars and lights and lots of people, but it made me nervous thinking about it. All I knew was that I wanted a chance, even if it was a small chance, at something better than what I had. And, from my recent experience of being out on my own with the cattle for several months took all doubt out of my mind that I really wasn't cared for very much by my grandmother and uncles. I was, more or less, their work girl. I couldn't read, I couldn't write, I knew no other language other than Somali. All I knew was the hard life of the village, and not even the life of the other girls there, but as hard, or harder, than even the boys. It seems, now that I look back, my prayers were answered the day we received that letter from my mother, as my life has never been the same since.

With permission from my grandmother and uncles, it didn't take me long to prepare to leave, as I didn't have many belongings other than my tire sandals, a skirt or two, and a covering for my head. I had no money and didn't even know where Kenya was or what Nairobi looked like, but I was willing and anxious to go and so ready to find a different future for myself. I was also very anxious to see my mother and meet the siblings I never had a chance to meet. Being a part of a family with brothers and sisters was one of my biggest dreams as it was the one thing I wanted the most

– to belong! But, I was also somewhat nervous to go, as I had only been with my mother for a few months when I was seven with malaria, and I wasn't sure how we'd get along. And now, here it was, right there for me. Most importantly, I was anxious to finally leave the criticism and poor treatment I received and the stern discipline of my grandmother. The truth is, I was afraid of her, as she was quick to whip me and yell at me - she was one tough chick!

It wasn't long, maybe a week or so, when the day came for us to leave. My uncle, Ahmed and grandmother took me to Beledwayne. It was very early in the morning when we left, before sunrise, so as to catch the bus. I'm not sure where my other uncles, Ali and Abdi were, or where Abdi's wife was, probably still sleeping just getting up in their own tent, but there were no good byes between us. So, we left before sunup and walked to the bus stop about twenty six miles away.

The walk to the bus was very nice. It took us the better part of the day walking along paths and donkey cart trails through the countryside. I'm glad Ahmed was there to take me; his voice was always so gentle, and we had some time to talk with each other as we walked. If it weren't for Ahmed, there wouldn't have been much love growing up in the village. I'll never forget his kindness, and not once did he raise his voice to me, except in his frustration when I lost the sheep in the river, and he had to jump in, in spite of the crocodiles, to save it. I think I would raise my voice as well in that situation!

We got to the bus stop in the afternoon and waited an hour or so for it to arrive, which it did, announcing itself by the plumes of dust we could see off in the distance as it sped towards us on the dirt road. I had my little bag in my hand and was wearing my one good dress, anxious to be going off to the big city.

The bus was full of people: mothers with children, old folks, young people, very crowded all going to the city as well. Beledwayne had been recaptured by its original tribe, and now it was safer to travel there. We got on, squeezing our way to a seat, Grandma and I in one, Ahmed in another, and off we went to Beledwayne which took about another three hours. I was beside myself, it all happening so fast and realizing I was leaving my life in the village forever. In a way, it was bitter sweet, as I wouldn't be seeing my favorite animals anymore, or walking the path down to the river to get water, or living in the simple life of the village.

Once we got there, we walked to the house of a friend of Ahmed's named Nabil where my grandmother and I stayed, while Ahmed stayed with another family due to lack of space at Nabil's house. We stayed there for about a week waiting for a cargo plane to come from Nairobi. There were no passenger planes in and out of Beledwayne, only ones that carried various kinds of cargo; if you could bribe the pilot, you could catch a ride to Nairobi, although it wasn't legal for him to do that. An aunt of mine in Nairobi paid a pilot for my passage, so that when he delivered his cargo to Beledwayne, he would transport me back to

Nairobi. So, we had to wait until his plane came having only a vague sense that it would be soon.

Staying there in Beledwayne was only the second time since I was seven that I had ever seen lights, cars, trucks, and regular houses - such a contrast from the country village I came from. Ahmed came to visit each day as we waited for plane to arrive. We had no money, so we couldn't do too much. I don't know why we couldn't have sold a sheep or goat to have some money, but we didn't; it didn't make any sense to me. Basically, we had nothing. I had nothing except for one dress that was not all worn out and torn up. I have to say I was disappointed as a young girl that they didn't buy me something a little nicer to wear. Many of the other girls my age had more attractive clothes, and I felt very self-conscious.

Finally, after a week or so, the plane landed with its load of khat, which is like tobacco with a stimulant in it. We met with the pilot who told us that he was returning to Nairobi the very next day. Early the next morning, Grandma, Ahmed and I got to the airport and found the plane and pilot. I said good bye to my grandmother and thanked her for all she'd done for me. A little selfishness crept in, as I also thought about how much I had done for her, but all I got was "Be good, Habibo." I then said good bye to Ahmed and climbed into the plane and looked back, I can still see him standing there, tall with his long robe and cheerful face. I didn't see him again until many years later.

There was another woman, a business woman, who needed to go to Kenya as well on the plane. So, it was just her and me and the pilot. This was my first time on an airplane; I was petrified and just knew we would crash before we got there. There were no seats or even a toilet, so we sat on the floor and had to hang on to some of the cargo bags as the flight got pretty bumpy at times with lots of turbulence, and the pilot was walking around in the plane on top of that. I thought, "Oh my goodness, I'm going to die soon." I think to help calm me down; the woman with me gave me a piece of gum – real gum which I had never had before in my life. I was only used to the gum you could get from certain trees and chew on that. The gum she gave me had two wrappers, which I did not understand. So I removed the outside paper wrapper and put the piece in my mouth – silver wrapping and all. It is so funny now that I look back on it. The lady scolded me saying, "No, you have to take the silver wrap off also, silly girl." I chewed it for a little while, but spit it out before too long - it still wasn't as good as the gum I'd find from trees.

After an hour or so, we had to stop at the border of Kenya and Somalia to fuel up, but the lady and I just stayed in the back of the plane, as we weren't even supposed to be on it. The landing was frightening; I thought the plane was going to burst apart or certainly run into some of the buildings as we were going so fast. However, we were OK. We took off again and flew for maybe another hour, then finally landed at a small airport in Nairobi around 5:00 in the afternoon - and it was raining very heavily.

At this time, with the civil war going on in Somalia, it was dangerous to cross country lines without transfer papers – very dangerous! If you were caught, you'd be put in jail with no way to get out except to bribe your way. Well, I had no papers with me to show the officials at the airport, so the woman I flew with agreed to say that I was her daughter and hopefully get me through the gates without any trouble. She said, "Just pretend you are with me."

We got off the plane and slipped in with some other people walking towards the airport pretending to be part of their group. It was a gated area with many uniformed men with guns standing all around, as security was high due to the war; I was so afraid. My old tapes started running, and I had this sinking feeling that, with so many men there, I'd get raped again. So, I just kept my eyes down and didn't look up at any of them. I felt their eyes on me and my memories came flooding back of fight or flight. I also felt they could just look at me and know that I was illegal, that it was maybe written all over my face. But, we made it through the gates and into the airport thanks to the woman I was with. I can't imagine how it would have been had I been all by myself. I'd have no idea where to go and, with no papers, I probably wouldn't have been allowed to even leave the gates. To top it off, I looked around the airport, as well as outside of it, and realized there was no one there to pick me up, of course, which is how my life always seemed to go.

The woman I was with, I'm sure, felt sorry for me, thinking, "What kind of a family is this child from?" To be perfectly honest, I kind of question the same thing myself. So, she told me she had friends there in Nairobi that I could stay with until we got hold of my mother. I agreed, having really no other choice. We waited and waited for a taxi, all wet, scared, cold, and tired. Finally it arrived, and we were in for one crazy ride. I thought the driver was a very poor driver, darting in and around traffic going so fast. Of course, I wasn't used to riding in a city. We took it through the streets of Nairobi which was much bigger than anything I'd ever seen or even imagined, and all so fast and busy. It was like being in another land. It was totally different than what I was used to - cement and tar, buildings with lights, cars and lots of traffic, people everywhere!

We finally arrived at the friend's house, and I was so glad. Providentially, the woman's friend was from our same tribe – the Hawaadle tribe, and, oddly enough, she knew my aunt that had arranged for my flight and her phone number. It's times like this when my faith is strengthened - when, against the odds, things work out. So, she called my aunt and told her I was there. The reason my aunt wasn't there to get me was that with having to bribe a pilot, you had no clue as to when the flight would be there, you just went when you could and hope you get where you needed to go.

I went to bed that night feeling very tired from the plane ride, the scare from the men with guns at the airport, then finally the taxi ride. And, I felt like I could puke from that gum. I needed to sleep really bad. They had a very nice house, very comfortable, with bunk beds and nice pillows. It was great. I guess it was the pillows that always impressed me when I went to the city. All I had was a rolled up piece of cloth or my arm to lay my head on. I remember they had a flush toilet which I had never seen before. In the village, we just went out into the bush to relieve ourselves. I didn't understand the flush part of the toilet. I have to confess, I took some underwear from the house as I needed some as I had to throw my underwear away because it was my time of the month. So, I threw my soiled underwear down the toilet and flushed. Well of course, it got all plugged up. I had to put my hand down the toilet to pull the underwear out. I never had to do anything like that before, it was disgusting!

I slept very well; it was the first time I'd been in a real bed since I was seven. You can imagine how I felt with clean sheets and blankets and a pillow - with a pillow case! It's funny what we take for granted, but really, these things, to many people in the world, are a major luxury which only very rich people get to enjoy. Once again, I find it odd that people complain when they have life so nice.

The next day, after much waiting, my aunt's husband came to get me, but it wasn't until about 11:00 at night that he arrived. I was scared, not really sure where we were going and not knowing this man. We drove for a ways, and he had to stop at a restaurant for some reason. He told me, "Wait here." So I stood in a corner, not being used to anything in a city or restaurants and not knowing what to do. It was full of men sitting around and eating and talking, many times looking over at me like I had just come from the bush country. I started to get really uncomfortable and felt like maybe the man abandoned me there. I wanted to run and somehow find my way back to my grandma's village. I was terrified! Finally, however, he came back. I remember thinking how hungry I was, but with no money, I couldn't buy any food. I was wishing I had some cow's milk with me.

When we finally arrived, my mother was waiting for me outside the gate in front of a blue colored hotel where she was staying. It was the first time I saw her in several years – I was very excited. She came out of the gate, and we were both overwhelmed with joy running to each other, hugging and kissing and crying. It was the most amazing feeling ever. She took me up to her room, and then we started talking and crying some more. I saw my little brothers and sisters: Naima four years old, Nura three, Halima two, and Mohamud five months old. I was so happy. I kissed and hugged them and lifted them up and played with them. We talked and visited until almost sunup, then, I slept until past noon.

Unfortunately, I was in for a shock, as life in Nairobi with my mother and brother and sisters was chaotic and tenuous, with the civil war in full force, as hundreds and thousands of families, men, women and their children, young people and old alike, flooded into Kenya escaping for their lives. I was expecting something like how my mother lived in Mogadishu, when I stayed with her there; however, the war changed all that. The city had swelled to more than twice its size, and people were moving about everywhere coming in from all over. We had no papers allowing us to be in the country and no money either. And, without papers, we had to hide all the time being very careful if we left the apartment so we didn't get caught. The police came every night knocking on doors and demanding to see papers, and if you had no papers, you were taken to jail, bribery being the only out. After a few weeks of living in secrecy and fear in my mother's motel room, she thought it would be best for us to leave Nairobi. I didn't realize we'd be going to a refugee camp, but my mother knew, and she knew it was probably our only option.

So, my mother and I and my four siblings packed up a few things and left one night around midnight when things in the city quieted down and there weren't as many soldiers and police around. We were so afraid of being caught, watching over our shoulders all the time, trying to carry the little ones as well as a few belongings. We took a taxi to the bus station, as we heard that a bus was leaving around 2:00 a.m. Thankfully, we got on the bus without any trouble.

We traveled on the bus the whole night. The children slept as much as they could, but the seats were close together and the bus crowded. We were all so tired with little or no sleep. Finally, the next morning, we got to Mombasa, the second largest city in Kenya. From there, we departed the bus and had to walk with the kids and our belongings to an old refugee camp called Utaango. It took us about three hours to get there. Utaango was a refugee camp that was about to be closed, I found out, and we were not going to be able to stay there, thank goodness! We were told there would be a bus leaving to take people to another camp, but we had to wait a day or so for it to leave.

Utaango was overcrowded and very, very unsanitary; it was really disgusting. We found a friend of my mother's living in a tent and we stayed with her for the day and night. The camp was built in a wet, rainy part of Kenya, much like a rain forest. It was very muddy with tents set up in the midst of the mud, with lots and lots of people, many sick and dying. It was so infested from all the people trying to live there. There was feces all around, rotten food, and the camp was full of cholera, hepatitis A, typhoid, malaria was a given, and children and old folks were dying every single day. Before we left Nairobi, we heard that Utaango was vile. We were told to be sure to buy socks at the second hand store before we got there, as there were worms crawling in the dirt that would try to burrow into the bottom of your feet, and the poor people, old and young alike were full of them. It was the absolute worst of life! So, se had to be sure to keep socks on the kids' feet to keep the worms from burrowing in.

That first night, my mother and brother and sisters slept inside the tent, and I and another lady had to sleep outside on the ground with the worms. I was so afraid of them, I'd try to wrap my feet with cloth and over my socks so they wouldn't burrow into my feet. All night long I barely slept.

We got up the next morning and found out that the buses weren't going to leave for another day, so we had to stay. It was one of the worst days of my life! Everything was wet and dirty, people coughing and sick and dying everywhere, little children stand-ing, sitting, staring with huge eyes and no muscle on their bones, large stomachs and nothing but sticks for legs. I was so worried that my brother and sisters and I would catch something. And, the constant threat of the worms burrowing into your feet was enough to make you crazy. It was something out of a very bad nightmare.

The next day we left, along with as many other peo-ple from the camp that could fit on the bus, and for two days we rode through the open grasslands to the other side of Kenya. I remember it was the most tiring, annoying, exhausting thing I had ever been through. Imagine being on a bus that was super crowded, trav-eling with four babies crying – lots of crying, lots of vomiting, lots of diarrhea, it was just unbelievable and being completely exhausted ourselves. We trav-eled for two days stopping only at night when the bus driver just pulled over in the desert and everyone got out and just slept on the ground wherever they could lay; I was so tired, dirty, hungry and worn out. It was like something out of a movie as we and these people were struggling for our lives, escaping a war ravaged country with no place to go. Every one of us had been uprooted from our homes with nothing to our name except for a few pieces of clothing and whatever we could grab fast and salvage. I could see the fear and fatigue in the faces of all the people. And, the poor children, having no idea what was happening or why. A very sad thing as we made our way to another refu-gee camp – the largest in the entire world!

Chapter Twelve

Dadaab

We arrived at Dadaab during the daytime. The camp was started in 1991 after General Barre was ousted from power, and everyone fled from Somalia. It has three main sites which were built to hold a total of 90,000 refugees, but by the time we got there in 1995, there were almost 150,000. Today, there are 460,000. I remember getting off the bus and looking out over the landscape; I could see thousands and thousands of people, tent after tent after tent all across the land which was flat and dusty, barren and wide open – nothing you could graze your animals on.

We got off the bus and stood in line with all the other people and finally were able to check in at the reception center manned by people from the United Nations. They took our names down and gave us a large tarp to make a tent, some corn, oil, flour, several plastic jugs for us to fill with water at one of the wells along with a little cart with wheel, and a few mattresses. The camp was divided into many sections in alphabetical order, and within each letter of the alphabet there were many subsections like, A-1, A-2, A-3 and so on to A 16 or 17, then B-1, B-2, B-3 all the way through the alphabet. Each subsection had about ten families in it with their tents set up about fifty feet from each other. We were assigned to section F-4. Unfortunately, the United Nations, who was running Dadaab, did not understand Somalia tribalism, and they mixed everyone together from many different tribes making for a rather tense situation.

We took our tent and food, carried the little ones and somehow, with all that, found our site to set up house. The first day was busy, going outside the camp to find branches and limbs as the inner structure for our tent as well as for fire wood, going to find water, meeting the people around us as well as taking care of the kids. A large makeshift fence surrounded the whole camp to keep marauders, rapists and robbers out. The fence was only made of limbs and branches from the trees in the area, and with a little effort, could be gotten through. Our tent site was near the big fence, so I had to go separate some of the branches to get outside of it in order to find branches and firewood so we could cook our meals. That night, we all just feel asleep so early being so tired from traveling for several days, taking care of the little ones, getting into the camp and finding our way through it, not to mention two days at Utaango. Soon, though, we got used to the camp.

Imagine being surrounded by thousands of other Somali men, women and children all having escaped their homeland trying to survive out in the middle of a vast barren land. I felt very intimidated at first, never having been around so many people in such a large area. Having come from the village and spending most of my life out herding animals pretty much by myself, I was overwhelmed by all the people. Many were from the cities of Somalia, more educated than me, more sophisticated. I felt very "less than" around them, and having to go about our business in the camp, I was pretty insecure. I had very little self-confidence and less self-esteem, so it stretched me somewhat to have to interact with all the people. However, we had to survive, and I did what I had to do.

When we first arrived, my mother asked me to go find out where to get water, so I asked some of the others in our section where to go. They directed me to a well about two miles away - one of the four wells provided for the whole camp where we'd walk sometimes daily, sometimes every other day, to fill up our containers. So, starting on the first day and every other day after that, I walked to the well closest to us which was about a half hour's walk away, pulling the little cart with our four water containers through the hot sand.

Each day, hundreds and hundreds of people would also be going to the well, so I had to start before dawn because the line would get very long. There were many fights in the line, mainly from women arguing and fighting over their place. Many times the fights would get very serious with knives and machetes, mainly because they would put their water tanks in front of each other or try to butt into line, and then the fights would break out and spread to whole families back in the camps with mothers, fathers, children and relatives fighting with some other family group; soon it would be one whole section of the camp against another, everyone with knives, sharp sticks or anything else they could find to hurt each other. Many times people were seriously hurt and had to be taken to the UN center for medical help. My best defense, however, was to not fuss with other people, and if they wanted to break into line in front of me, I'd let them. For three years I dealt with that precarious line, never quite sure when a fight would break out as tempers flared and patience with life became scarce.

After getting our water, I'd make breakfast for us, usually we'd have bread made out of the flour, water, and a little oil that we were given, and water to drink, or sometimes we'd have ground corn and make a flat corn pancake out of it. Sometimes, I'd trade the corn with the neighbors for a little tea, as bartering was how we could survive as very few people had any money to buy anything. We'd also have a type of pasta which I'd make from flour, water, oil and perhaps some milk from the powdered milk we'd get from the UN center or from trading with one of the neighbors if we had anything that day to actually trade.

We'd wash the few cups or dishes that we had in a bucket, or rather rinse them because all we had for soap was big bars cut from a large soap block. Our kitchen, being outside our hut, was made like a small cubby with bushes around it on three sides to keep the dust and sand out. For a fire pit, we had three rocks placed so that we could build a fire in the middle; we'd place our pots or pans on top of the rocks and then cook our food.

So I cooked all our food outside – for three years – which wasn't so unusual for me, as we always cooked our meals outside in the village, and I didn't know any different. Sometimes my mother would be with us, sometimes not, as she'd often travel back to Nairobi trying to find money from relatives and friends while I'd be left to look after the little ones.

Laundry we did by hand three times per day in cool water, sometimes we'd have a bar of soap, sometimes not. The kids had diarrhea the whole time we were there, so laundry was a daily issue. They weren't bars of soap like in America or western countries, but bars rough cut from a big slab which would then be cut up into smaller pieces. To dry the clothes, I'd string a line between the branches of the bushes around us and hang the clothes there to dry. The clothes the kids had were called "hudhay" or second hand stuff - some colored T shirts, no socks or underwear. Older kids would have sandals made out of old tires; younger kids went barefoot.

The kids didn't have much to do to occupy their time. Usually they'd play in the sand around our tent, maybe with some empty bottles or sticks or rocks or an occasional scorpion! There were other children in our camp, of course, who my siblings would play with as well. They were like nothing was wrong and life consisted of living in the camp with some friends next door. They didn't know any different. Our camp and the camps around us became, to us, a little neighborhood within a large, large city. Many sections of it I never did see, as it wasn't always safe to wander off by yourself, and it was so extremely large.

Health issues were very prevalent – malaria, pin worms, tape worms, malnourishment – all part of daily life. Some of the children had cholera, sores and infections, feet cut and sore, my legs were always cut and sore, to this day, I have the scars to show it. Scorpions were abundant and all of us were bitten on a regular basis. If we were bit, there were no doctors to take us to, so we'd just wrap the sore/bite and wait until it went away.

Living there was always riddled with problems. Picking up supplies once per month, flour, corn and oil, fights would always break out. It was common for fights to occur with knives and someone getting killed.

One of the biggest problems we had after awhile was finding firewood outside the camp. With so many people, all needing to cook by making a fire, soon the supply in the immediate vicinity of the camp was depleted. We'd have to go out in the bush to find them, which we would do during the daytime, never at night as it was dangerous out there, and we'd usually go in groups of three or four, many times walking quite a few miles to find wood. The longer we were there, the farther out we had to walk to find firewood. There were always men and boys hiding outside the camp, living outside the camp, who would live off of those within the camp. They'd try to rob you or rape you or sometimes even kill you. We'd often, every week, hear of these kinds of tragedies happening, but mainly if someone wasn't thinking and went out by themselves, then they were easy prey. There were no police anywhere to be found, so the people were their own law.

At night we could hear the animals howling outside the fence - hyenas and a kind of large cat called a "duwaco" - and an occasional gun shot or scream. The animals would growl out in the bushes; we could all hear it and hope it wouldn't get into our camp. The kids would be afraid at night, so I'd sleep with them very close to me trying to comfort them and reassure them that the animals wouldn't get into our camp, although inside I wasn't so sure. Also, at night, we were all afraid because some of the "slichers" as we would call them – men and boys with guns and knives – would come in through the fence and go into tents and rape people and take jewelry or anything of value and even sometimes kill people. We'd hear guns popping and get news the next morning that they were in this camp or that camp; luckily, they were never seen in our camp. Many times in the night if I really needed to relieve myself, I couldn't go because I was afraid of going out and walking around in the bushes that they might be around and kidnap or rape me - I was very afraid of that! Oddly enough, this wasn't so much of an adjustment for me, because all my life I and the other girls in the village had to be on guard for rape. I went through it all the time being a nomad being one of the only girls herding the animals out in the grasslands.

Once each week for the whole time we were there, all the children in the whole camp had to be taken to the UN center located in the middle of the camp to be weighed and checked for diseases. Our section of Dadaab, F-4, was to go on Wednesdays, which we did each week. I remember so clearly carrying my one year old brother, Mohammed, and two year old sister, Sarah, one on my back and the other in front using a thin cloth tied in a knot over my shoulder as a sling, to the main building. Unfortunately, they being plagued by diarrhea, it many times was a mess just to get to the center. It was about two miles away from our tent, and I had to walk through the hot sand so deep my feet would sink in making it very hard to walk. I'd make this trek twice a week where UN volunteers from other countries would poke Sarah and Mohamed's fingers to check their iron levels and then weigh them trying to keep ahead of malnutrition. They'd give us cookies, crackers and also, based upon their weight, additional dried milk, oil, corn and rice to take back to our camp, which we were so grateful for as we had nothing to our name. In spite of the treks to the UN center and the additional food, my brother and sisters became malnourished anyway, as did most of the other children in Dadaab, all ending up with that refugee look of large stomachs, thin legs and sad eyes.

On the way to the UN center, I'd pass other huts, many of them, hundreds of them, with children playing outside in the sand wearing a small t-shirt if they were fortunate, but most were simply bare naked. The look of malnutrition was the norm, as was hopelessness on the faces of their parents, mainly mothers, as fathers would be away either fighting in the war, or trying to make some money in the larger cities. It was that look of hopelessness in their mother's eyes, and the sadness in the children's, that haunts me even to this day. Everyone, including myself, had been uprooted from their homes, villages, and cities where life was pretty well set up, even if we were dirt poor.

For us refugees, home was now living in a tent city on a vast flat plain having no animals, very little clothing, no work and no purpose, as the turbulence in our country seemed to only be getting worse with no hope of any centralized government to pull the country together. Within Dadaab, in an effort to find some semblance of normalcy, order, and protection, many of the people were beginning to gather together amongst their own tribes and clans just like what was happening in greater Somalia where the country was falling back into tribalism – everyone fighting with everyone!

I was in Dadaab for three years. Sadly, I consider that time a step up from village life, as well as a step in the right direction in improving my life. I didn't know, however, whether I'd get ever out of Dadaab, or if I'd spend my life there as many have done and are still doing. During my stay in the camp is when I learned the alphabet and basic math. Although we did not have money to go to school, I would borrow my friend's homework so I could learn what they learned, and once I learned how to read, I was hooked on it for life. It was a big turning point for me.

The expectation for me and my life had always been, "Oh you're supposed to do this - grow up as a girl, find a husband, get married and have kids." I wasn't really in search of an education and a career. I thought I was OK, and that pretty soon I would get married and get out of my mother's tent and have my own tent. I honestly thought I would remain in Dadaab for the rest of my life with a husband and children and our own tent. My thoughts of returning to Somalia were gone, as the whole country was in complete chaos, and in many ways still is.

I've told many people that it was faith that got me out of my grandmother's village, and out of Somalia, and out of the Dadaab, and usually they will ask, "Well, how did faith get you out of there?" I tell them that if you have no plans to do something, but all of a sudden an opportunity pops up and the things that happen are the best in your entire life. When things like that take place, that many times are out of your control and your life changes completely, that would be as a result of faith; faith that who you pray to is helping you and has your best interests in mind. How then does faith come in when bad things happen? Well, we know that sometimes bad things force us to cry out and ask for help, which in turn increases our faith when we do get help.

My chances of leaving Dadaab were very slim, I guess one in one hundred and fifty thousand. Out of thousands and thousands of people, all needing help - many of them more than me - why was I picked? And, the population of Dadaab was increasing every single day. I can only say that for all of us, there's a bigger plan that most times we're unaware of, but we need to be ready when those opportunities are laid in front of us. And, when we are given opportunities, we have an obligation to give it our very best out of appreciation.

Chapter Thirteen

Rescued by Providence

——•═══•——

Leaving Dadaab all started with my cousin, Hawo, who came to the camp before me by approximately three years. She and her husband and children escaped to the camp in 1992, having fled from Somalia like all the rest of us. She, however, came from the city, Mogadishu, and was more savvy than I. It was her savvy that helped me eventually leave Dadaab and come to America.

Sometimes I'd go to her hut across the camp and help her with her kids and spend time there, maybe even spend a few nights, while my mother watched my siblings. We'd talk all the time about how it would be so nice to get out of Dadaab, to maybe get back to our lives the way they used to be. But all the talk in the camp was about going to America where there would be a better chance at creating a good life. The big hope for everyone, man, woman and child, was to get chosen to come to America. Hawo and I would fantasize about how rich we'd be and live in fine homes with nice clothes. To me, though, they were just fantasies as I thought my chances were so slim, like winning the lottery, why should I even try?

Twice per year, people in the camp could fill out an application to come to the United States, unfortunately, only about one hundred got picked each time. So, each year, two hundred people, out of one hundred and fifty thousand, would be chosen. The process, from start to finish took about one year from the time you apply to when you actually got on the plane to leave for America.

During this time, as Hawo and I would talk and dream of something better than life in a refugee camp, we'd see people who found out they were selected to go. They would actually almost go out of their minds with happiness. They'd scream and yell and dance and cry all at the same time, so filled with joy – and hope. I've seen them fall down on their knees, their face on the ground, crying thanks and praises for prayers being answered. It was extremely moving. Others, who were not selected, were equally moved, only in the other direction – sad, depressed, hopeless, frustrated, afraid, filled with despair!

Late in the summer of 1998, when Hawo said to me, "Habibo, we need to apply to go to America, it is time to leave this camp." So, we applied. My mother applied as well for her and my siblings. But I applied independently, while Hawo applied with her husband and children. We put the paperwork in about July, just like thousands of others with the same hopes as us. We pretty much forgot about the application and went back to our daily routines. We didn't really think our chances were very good of being selected.

Having applied, we'd check each day at the UN center to see if the list of those selected had been posted yet. They'd post it inside a gated area on an open door, taping it to the door. Every day, people would go and check for their ID number to see if it was up on the paper. If it was there, that meant you've been picked for processing. And, if your ID was not there, then you could try again the next time and the next time and the next, for as many years as you cared to apply - I imagine there are people there to this day that are still trying! Several weeks after we applied, Howa went to see if the list was up yet; normally, it was posted by Thursday or Friday.

I remember it was Thursday afternoon, a day I'll never forget. I was staying with Hawo children, three of whom were napping and one was out playing around. She went to check at the center again to see if we were selected; she always felt positive that we'd be chosen. I, however, had my doubts. Out of thousands of people, why would we be selected, is what I thought?

I was sitting outside her tent watching her youngest son play in the sand, when all of a sudden she came screaming back to the tent just ecstatic, jumping up and down, screaming, yelling, happier than I'd ever seen her. "Habibo, Habibo, we were selected! We were selected!"

I was shocked. I said, "Selected? Are you sure?"

"Yes, yes, we were selected, Habibo, we're going to America, we're going to America."

I realized she meant it, no one could be that excited and that filled with joy and not mean it. It hit me, and I started screaming and jumping up and down with her and crying, hugging each other, we were so happy.

Right away, I thought about my mother, and I wanted to run and tell her the good news. So, I told Hawo that I had to run and tell my mom. I ran off towards our tent; I remember running and being worried whether she would let me go or not. I didn't know how it was going to go with her, because here I was, a young single girl with no relatives in America, or even any friends; plus I had to help her take care of my siblings as well. I didn't know if she'd let me out of that commitment. But, I thought to myself, "I want to go, I need to go to America and make lots of money and just take me out of this shit hole!" So I ran as fast as I could to our camp - jubilant, ecstatic, giddy with happiness.

My mother was sitting outside our tent holding Mohamud and watching the other kids play with the neighbors in the sand. I ran up to her and said, "Mom, Mom guess what? We won, Hawo and I won the lottery, we won the lottery, oh my gosh."

My mom, trying to make some sense out of it, saying, "What are you talking about, to America? Habibo, settle down, settle down, tell me." I could barely speak, "We won the lottery! Oh my gosh, I'm included in this, can I go, can I go? I want to go there, I want to work, I want to help you, I want to send you money?"

And my mom answered, "You know what, Habibo? Sure, why not, I trust you. You need to go to America."

I was so happy, so excited. I learned then what it felt like to win the jackpot. Can you imagine how I felt, after living in a primitive village all my life, herding animals, being a nomad, hiding in bushes and trees so not to get raped by camel boys - and then living in a refugee camp for three years? I can tell you, it's a feeling you'd never forget - and I never will!

This was the first time I ever seriously thought about the reality of going to America. Before this, we'd say that we were filing out this paperwork to go to America, and we'd submit it just like everyone else, kind of part of our routine. I had no clue that it actually would happen. My mother was so encouraging to me, I was kind of surprised. She told me that it was time for me to do more with my life, to try and make something of myself. She said there were many opportunities in America and that I was a smart girl. She'd say, "Habibo, you can do this. You can make a better life for yourself." Unfortunately, she and my siblings weren't selected, and never were to this day. But, she never let on that she was disappointed or envious. She was only very excited for me. This is where I've seen greatness in my mother. I've seen it at other times also – her great strength. This is why I love her so much.

A week or so went by, and from the notices posted at the UN center, we found that the first part of the process was to begin. A date was set for all those selected to go to the center and begin. We were so filled with anticipation, however, the anxiety of the unknown also crept in. I realized I was going off all by myself knowing no one. I didn't know whether I'd have the skills or not to make it in America. All I knew was how to herd sheep and goats and cows.

We went to the center on the day appointed and waited in a long line. Everyone in the line was happy and excited, like new life was breathed into them. It took the whole day long, because there were a lot of people there. We stood all morning as the line moved very slowly. At high noon, the UN workers doing the screening took their lunch break while the line was still there, they took almost two hour hours, and then came back while the whole time we stood in the line. Fortunately, we were told to bring some food and water with us, because once we got into the gate, we weren't able to come out if being screened for the process.

The volunteers took our fingerprints and picture, wrote down our information, and then let us go. Then, the next day, we'd go back, and they'd ask the same questions that we had written down and go through more questions and more questions and more questions. They would ask things like "Why do you want to go to the United States?" One of the lady volunteers asked me, I remember, "Why did I want to go?"

I responded, "I want to work, go to school and help my mom."

She asked me, "Have you ever been to school or if I was in school now?

I told her, "No, I could never afford that."

She then asked me, "Habibo, have you ever been afraid, or have you ever seen anything horrifying or bad?"

Her question hit me like a brick wall. I broke down and started crying right there in front of her, because here was this total stranger talking to me like no one has ever talked to me before. No one had ever asked me about my feelings, about things, incidents that have changed my life. She wanted to know if I've experienced anything that was distressing.

I said, "Yes, I have. I have seen people get killed-brutally; twice I've seen women being raped in front of me, once when I was about four and then a few years later when I was out looking after the goats in a distant part of the country." I told her of the abuse at the hands of older relatives and fending off the camel boys – successfully and unsuccessfully - while out living as a nomad. I told her I also saw things when civil war was happening in 1993; how many of the young boys and men that I knew were killed or maimed or lost eyes and limbs. I told her about how we'd try to nurse them back to health, if we could!

I also talked about the desperate state my mom and little brother and sisters were in because of being so very poor and not able to afford things, very small things that Americans take for granted. I didn't realize how much I was going on about our lives, but her question just triggered a whole flood of feelings and frustrations within me. I told her everything. She looked at me, right into my eyes, and said, "You know what, Habibo. I'm going to do everything in my power to make sure that you live that life that you dream of, and that you get an education, and that someday you feel safe." I told her, "Thank you, thank you so much," and I meant it from the bottom of my heart.

Two of my best friends who lived near our camp were mad at me, because they went through the same process, but after being selected and interviewed, they failed the interview and were found not eligible to go. Their father said to my mom, "Oh Gotacheka, you cannot send your daughter, she's just a teenager, she's too young. You don't want her to go over there. She's going to turn into a Christian, she's going to get a lot of influence. I would not advise you to allow that."

I remember my mom answering, "Listen, I trust my daughter, she's very smart, and I'm going to let her go."

I passed my interview as did my cousin, Hawo; we were unbelievably emotional and so happy. A couple weeks later, another posting said we would be leaving Dadaab in about one week - never to return! We were to take a bus and go to Nairobi, where we would get our medical examinations done. It was at that moment that it really hit me. I was going away to another place, that I didn't know, and I wouldn't be coming back. I would be leaving my little brother and sisters, my mother, the village, my grandma and uncles – all of it!

I had no idea what to expect in America. I didn't know what was going to happen to me, but at that point I made a commitment to myself to go and work and try to give us a better life. I knew I was going to give it my best. You see, we had no TV's or computers, no magazines, catalogs, newspapers or anything to show us what America was like. We only heard that it was full of money and riches, that people were wealthy beyond imagination, and that it was available for all to have. I literally thought there would be money everywhere just flowing from windows. There were times I felt scared, sad, afraid, but I had to be brave; I knew it was something I had to do.

Before leaving Dadaab and taking buses to Nairobi, all of us that were chosen had to gather at a gated, guarded, fenced in area which was really just a piece of land, wide open, with a few trees, almost like what you'd see livestock kept in. Hawo, her family and I, along with the others selected were sequestered in that gated area, so as to be ready to go when the buses came the next day, but also so that there wouldn't be any mistakes or mixups with people going that hadn't been approved.

So, on a hot Wednesday afternoon, they had us all go in there and locked us in. It felt odd to be locked in, but no one cared, we were so anxious and happy to have been chosen for a new life. I remember the day like it was yesterday: it was hot and so sticky with very little shade; everyone was in everyone else's face right out in the hot sun. We had water, but no where to go to the bathroom. If you had to relieve yourself, you just went over by the fence, no privacy, nothing - men, women, children, boys, and girls – and you just relieved yourself right there. I have to say, it was very demeaning right out there in the open in front of everybody, but what would you do in that situation? Put up a fuss? Demand better conditions? You'd probably just go along with it as we did.

As night fell, we all had to sleep there as well, curled up on the ground near people we knew, families together, waiting for the night to pass, the sun to rise and the buses to come and take us away. We all knew it was going to be that way, but it wasn't very pleasant. However, we were willing to do anything - anything in order to come to America! I was used to sleeping on the ground, so it wasn't such a new experience for me. But those from the cities, you could tell it was difficult for them. At least there was a locked fence, which, for once, allowed us to sleep without fear of being robbed and raped.

Early in the morning, shortly after sunrise, the UN volunteers returned to the camp with several large buses. They came and woke us up, unlocked the gate and had us all get into the buses. It was an exciting time as things started to move, as we all knew that life had smiled on us, and we were off to a new life.

The ride to Nairobi was a long one, taking a whole day riding across Kenya raising all kinds of dust behind us with the bus crowded, kids excited, all of us eager. I had plenty of time to look out the window and think about my life and what strange turn of events were occurring. I realized I wouldn't be seeing this landscape for quite some time, if ever. I thought a lot about my grandmother and Ahmed along with my life in the village. I remembered the crocodiles, hiding in the woods at night from neighboring tribes trying to invade our village. I remembered the bouts I had with malaria, and the worst of my life, being out on my own with the cows as a nomad. It all seemed like it happened such a long time ago.

We finally arrived in Nairobi at nightfall; the area in the city they took us to was called Iselee, and is still there to this day. Here in America, you'd call it a ghetto or slum or worse than a ghetto. It was, and still is, a disgusting place with garbage everywhere in the streets. It was raining when we got there, making it all the worse. The place was filled with homeless children, drug addicts, alcoholics and all kinds of the worst type of people, many sleeping right there in the streets. The muddy streets were the most foul smelling thing you could imagine, where, literally, your leg would sink into the much almost to your knee, and if you didn't pull your clothing up, it got covered with mud and human waste.

They put us all in motels in this area, and, unfortunately, this is where we had to stay for about two months while we went through all sorts of medical exams and orientation classes in Nairobi waiting for our flights to leave. It was horrifying! I rarely saw a large city, much less this part of a large city. Walking in the Isalee area was dangerous, and all my fears came back to me as well as my defenses. People would throw things at us and chase us, some would yell as we walked by, but I had to just keep walking and ignore them. It was sad to see what level of life they had sunken into – worse than the beasts in the wild.

Each day, we had to take buses to downtown Nairobi to have our medical checkups. We'd be gone all day, waiting in lines, having vitals taken, various blood and stool and urine tests, teeth looked at, Xrays, and many vaccinations given. Up to this point, I had never had a vaccination; I didn't even know what they were. Start to finish, it took us a week to get everyone taken care of.

The following week we had orientation to go to. Each day, we'd take a bus and ride three hours out of Nairobi to a center set up to prepare refugees for their transition to new countries. We would leave at 5:00 am and wouldn't get back until 6:00 or 7:00 at night. They explained all sorts of things to us in a classroom setting: the legal system in America; some basic English phrases like, "Where is the rest room?" "Thank you." "Please." "What is the time?" "Where am I?" And, we were told what to do and what not to do to try to fit into western culture. We were told not to be starting fights or picking arguments with people. We were told to be careful in inner cities and to mind our own business. And we were told about the 911 system. There was a big misconception among us over calling 911, because a lot of the kids were saying, "I can call 911 if my parents yell at me, and the police will come and protect me." And the parents were thinking, "Oh my God, I'm not going to America, because my kids will call 911 on us." It's funny now looking back on it. They taught us about what to expect when we first arrived in America describing the various states we'd be going to and the weather, and how to be prepared for that. And, they gave us a book about all these different things. I didn't speak any English, nor could I read it, so I just left my book in Nairobi.

When orientation was complete, we simply waited at our hotels for our flights to leave. One by one, the members of our group left, some flights left within a few days, others had to wait their turn. We'd all go and look at the lists to see when our name came up to leave. For me, I stayed there a total of about two months waiting for my flight. The UN volunteers gave us some money to buy ourselves food and things that we needed; I was especially frugal with mine, so that I wouldn't run out as I had no idea how long before I'd be leaving. Some of the others in our group spent theirs right away on clothes, perfume, jewelry, thinking they were already rich. However, they soon learned that they were back in poverty asking everyone if to share their money with them.

Before long, my roommate left on her flight; after that, I had the hotel room to myself. All of a sudden, I was alone. My room was quiet; I had no responsibilities; I did not live in fear; and there was not so much stress in my life. I had no children to take care of, no animals to herd, no water and food to get and haul back to our tent, no responsibilities. I had some distant relatives in the area, so I'd go visit with them and spend some time there. It was very different being all alone with no family. Hawo and her family had already left for America, and I believe she went to California. I just had myself. It was a time when I was finally able to be a young woman, sleeping in each morning, basically just taking care of myself and having some fun. I even found some time to mingle with boys.

One of my friends from Dadaab came to visit me, and we had lots of fun. Her cousin, who was with us in the camp, was just gaga over me. He was like, "Oh, my gosh, I want to marry you. I don't want you to leave." He even bought me a really nice necklace. However, before I was selected to go to America, he didn't even acknowledge me, didn't even talk to me. I realized he was only acting like this because I was going to America, and he wanted me to send him money. I thought, "I don't think so!"

Each day after I got up, my routine included checking the lists that were hung in the hotels to see if and when my flight would be leaving. Day after day, other names would appear, but not mine. Finally, around the first week of August, I went to see if my name was on the list, and sure enough, there it was. It said I was going to travel on the 27th of August. I got so excited and nervous, almost sick to my stomach with anxiety – the time had come to leave Africa and go to America!

My mother, learning when I was to leave, brought my brother and sisters to Nairobi, so we could spend some time together. They stayed with my step dad's sister, who also lived in Nairobi. She owned a house with three bedrooms: one bedroom for her and her two daughters; another for her two boys; and another for my mom and siblings – one room with two mattresses for the five of them, that was it. There was nothing else. There was one bathroom outside the house and no kitchen. So, if my mom wanted to cook, she'd go outside to her little stove that the woman lent to her and cook what she could. While waiting for my flight, I would go and help my mom with the kids; that's when it hit me the most as to how hard she was struggling having no money and no help with the kids. One time, she made some porridge out of corn, and we didn't have anything to eat with it – no milk, no soup, nothing. I realized then that I really had to come to America, so I could get my mom and little brother and sisters out of there and help them out.

As the day approached for my flight to leave, others were going shopping, buying clothes, getting all excited to go to America. I didn't have any money to buy clothes, but I did have a skirt and a blouse and a long dress with two or three kamats (head coverings). I had two gifts from different people and a small piece of luggage that one of my distant aunts lent me. I had one little ear ring that my mom bought me once, and I gave that back to her saying, "Mom you keep this, I'm going to America, and I can buy one there. You keep this, you need it more than I do."

The day we were to leave was a sad one, as I realized I wouldn't be seeing my mother or brother and sisters for quite some time. The flight was scheduled to leave at eight o'clock at night, but I had to be there at 5:00, so that they could process us and secure us inside the gated area - again. By this time, I was used to being put inside a gated area, it reminded me of my goats and sheep and cows who had to go into their corral each night so they wouldn't wander off. That whole day, I was so nervous; I couldn't eat, I had diarrhea, and I couldn't sleep the night before. I was a mess, but I was showing a brave face; I did not show any fear whatsoever. UN volunteers came for us to take us to the airport; it was time to leave. I kissed my mother goodbye and my little sisters and brother. I hugged them all for a long time as I knew I wouldn't be feeling their arms around my neck for quite a while. I got into the van with two other families, waved goodbye and didn't look back. It was a very sad scene, but I didn't want to cry. I wanted to be strong...for mama and my siblings...because I was to get them a better life. My mom said to me, "Habibo, be very strong and stay positive. Trust yourself, and somehow you will find a way and meet nice people."

Chapter Fourteen

Goodbye Africa, Hello America

———◆•◆•◆———

Our plane left the Nairobi airport at three in the afternoon - destination Amsterdam. It was a city I had never heard of and couldn't imagine where it was or what it looked like. Little did I know, that it was one of the centers of the western world as well as where most international flights come in and out of. I remember thinking how the plane was so large, I couldn't imagine how it would get off the ground, being a whole lot more than the little cargo plane I took from Beledwayne to Nairobi three years earlier. It had three seats across, then the aisle and three more seats – and seatbelts! It takes riding in a cargo plane on burlap bags of khat, worrying about being tossed across the floor because of the turbulence, to appreciate the seats in a regular commercial airplane.

When I got settled into my seat, it really hit me hard, that I was going to another world; a world that I didn't know a thing about, with people I didn't know either. I didn't even know the language! I left my mother, grandmother, uncles, friends, animals, and the only life I ever knew behind. No more swimming in the river, no more grazing the animals out on the grasslands, no more fearing for my life or having to fight off camel boys or listening to the criticisms of my uncle, Abdi, or the harshness of my grandmother. Even with all that, I started to panic, thinking I wanted to get off the plane and go back to my grandmother's village, even though that was exactly what I was praying to leave. I thought, "What am I getting into, maybe I'm in way too deep – way over my head?" But, the plane doors were closed and locked, and we were already backing out of the airport - there was no turning back now! So, I thought, "America, here I come."

I remember feeling so emotional, excited, scared, nervous, anxious all at the same time. But I also felt somewhat numb, like I was in a dream. The plane was full of other Somalis - many refugees and some that were just flying out of Nairobi. I don't know what I was coming down with, but by the time the plane was ready to take off, I was starting to feel sick and feverish and getting a dry hacking cough – probably something I picked up in Nairobi. Then, to make matters worse, the food we were given on the plane was so disgusting to me. It was some kind of a hot dish (you can tell I live in Minnesota – hot dish) with bread, some sauce and a glass of soda. I wasn't used to that sort of thing. I was used to dried rice, boiled or fried meat, beans, and milk cooked outside over an open fire. I had much to get used to when it came to modernized food. I realized that I would probably never be eating like that again over an open fire outside a hut.

We arrived in Amsterdam around 10:00 a.m., and the UN people were right there at the gate waiting to help us refugees as we got off the plane. There were several of them all smiling, holding up welcome signs. Each one took about twenty of us to the cafeteria to feed us. I didn't recognize any of the food and had no idea what to get – so many choices of foods I didn't even know what they were. I had never seen a hamburger, or fries, or hot dogs. What's Coke, Sprite, Pepsi? And, what on earth is Ketchup? So, I just got an orange drink, when really I could've had anything I wanted. I've had orange juice before from living out in the village, but I'd just pick some oranges out of the tree and squeeze my own, but this stuff was nothing like that. To me, it tasted so artificial, nothing like what I was used to. But, I had no room to complain; it was given to me for free. I had to remind myself that just a few months before, I was living in the largest refugee camp in the world.

We only had to wait three hours in Amsterdam for our flight to New York. Before I knew it, we were leaving the second continent that I stood foot on in less than twenty four hours, and we were off to a third one – North America! Even though I was feeling sick and feverish, I was beside myself with excitement, as were all the other refugees on the plane. We had visions of being rich, very rich! Thinking there would be money flowing everywhere in America. What we didn't realize, however, was how hard one has to work for it, until we got here!

The plane ride was very long - about nine hours. We left around 11:00 p.m., and I was getting sicker and sicker all the time, at a time when I should have been feeling my best. I could barely walk, had a terrible headache, and was vomiting every half hour or so in the little restroom at the back of the plane and running a fever. A lot of that, I'm sure, was nerves.

I experienced a lot by this time in my life, but I have to say, flying off by myself to a strange land with no one there to pick me up at the airport or help me find my way in the United States, was very, very stressful. What gave me courage, rather than screaming with fright, was the thought that I had to do it for my mother and brother and sisters. It gave me a purpose and a job to do – that's the only thing that kept me going. If it weren't for that, I don't think I could've done it. Somehow when we do things for others, especially things that are difficult or fearsome, we gather courage, whereas, if we do it for ourselves, it seems much harder.

Finally, when I didn't think I could sit in my seat any longer, the pilot announced that we were approaching New York City. I looked out the window, and I was astonished. I had never seen so many bright lights in my life; the whole sky, and as far as I could see, was filled with lights, lots of lights shining so bright and reflecting off the water, the whole sky lit up as if it was filled with diamonds and jewels. It was the most beautiful sight I've ever seen in my life! And all the sky scrapers! I couldn't believe buildings could be made so tall. I thought right then and there, America truly is a very, very, very rich country. In the village and in Dadaab, there were no lights, not even electricity, and nothing but huts, so you can imagine how it looked to me?

From the airport, we took a bus to our hotel. I remember crossing a bridge and looking out over the water at the New York skyline. It was breathtaking; I knew I was a long, long way from the grasslands of Somalia. It was a long bus ride to the hotel, seeming like it took hours and hours. I just tried to sleep, but was so excited; it was hard not to keep looking out the windows. In fact, everyone on the bus was way beyond tired after such a long trip, but very excited as well to be here.

The hotel we were brought to was just beautiful – it had sheets and blankets and pillows, and it smelled great; I had never seen soap and shampoo and conditioner much less little bottles of them. I had never seen such luxury before - and the pillows! For someone that never slept with a pillow, that was the ultimate! There were even extra pillows and blankets in the closets. There were four of us that stayed in the hotel room together, three other women and myself - I was the youngest.

It's hard to imagine how this all appeared to us, coming from a refugee camp where people broke in through the fence made of branches and sticks to rob you and rape you, where hyenas could be heard howling at night, where babies and children were dying from malaria and starvation, where the rest room was a spot in the dirt. We were saved, is how it felt. It was a very humbling experience, with much reflection about, "Why me? How have I deserved this? And, what sort of kindness is this to bring us this long way and help us like this?" Very humbling indeed!

We woke up in the morning to one of the women saying, "Let's go, we have to go, hurry up." So we got up and didn't even have time to clean up. I quickly washed my face and brushed my teeth, a little bewildered over the tooth paste and tooth brush, as I had never used either before. In Somalia, we use a brush made from the branches of the Roomay tree rubbed against our teeth. I remember thinking the tooth paste was really disgusting, foaming and frothing in my mouth; I'm used to it now and like it, but the first time was a very odd experience. I have to say, I still finish my teeth with a Roomay tree stick – very refreshing. I wore the same clothes I left home in, really having nothing else to change into, and rushed out of the hotel room.

We were shown to the hotel breakfast area; I had juice and a sweet roll – I've never seen anything like that before, either, but it was good. Quickly after breakfast, we were off to the airport again to catch yet another plane - this time to Dallas. Only a certain number of us were to go to Dallas and on to Phoenix, while others were distributed to different parts of the country; some went to Virginia, some Nebraska, some Ohio, California, North Carolina, and Minnesota.

We again waited in the gated area for our flight. I imagine we were quite a sight, all dressed in our Somali garbs and head coverings, none of us speaking the language, and looking like we were always lost. This time, however, I was ready for the plane ride. I especially wanted a window seat, so I could see this land called America. We flew during the daytime, which was great, as I had a chance to look out over the countryside of America. It was very pretty! I could see the lakes and rivers, fields of different kinds of crops, small towns and cities way below us. It all seemed so orderly with roads criss-crossing the country side, and fields of crops laid out in nice patterns. It was a wonderful feeling for a young girl. As we were about to land, we flew above the Dallas. Looking out over the city, I thought, "So this is America!"

From Dallas we took yet another plane on to Phoenix, which was just a short ride. When we landed, social workers met us there, holding up pieces of paper with our names written on them. I thought it was so funny, that they'd do that; it worked though.

The social worker took three of us females, myself and two older women, to an apartment where we were to live, but he first took us to a food store in Phoenix to buy some supplies. He brought us into the grocery store, and we just stood there staring – like we'd say here in America, "Like deer in the headlights." None of us had ever seen such a thing. We were used to buying our food in small little open markets at best. But here it was, huge and inside a building, and more food and stuff than anything we had ever seen in our whole lives. To us it was opulent, wealth beyond belief, so much food and so many choices. We had no idea what to buy or even where to begin. Our social worker told us to go and get whatever we wanted. He didn't realize, that we didn't even know where to start or what to look for. We were in a major cultural shock; hardly able to move or look around the store; which direction would we go first, the produce aisle? What's that?

Believe it or not, I got a large carrot cake and some orange juice. Can you believe it? A carrot cake! To this day, every time carrot cake is served, I have to laugh inside remembering my first choice of food; of all the food available at the store, I chose a carrot cake. One of the other women got a big bag of oranges. The social worker spoke in Arabic, which I understood a little of. He said, "Is that all you're going to get?" I told him, I didn't know what to get. He just said, "OK." And he paid for the food and we left.

Looking back now, there were so many other things that would have been better for me than carrot cake, such as fruit or some chicken or milk and bread. In fact, the social worker was expecting us to stock up for our apartment; however, I believe he was in a culture shock as well. Perhaps he thought we really liked carrot cake and oranges. But we were completely out of our element and didn't have any idea how to get what we needed. The store just completely blew us away. It would have been nice if the man guided us through that and helped us pick out some things, or better yet, just have some basics stocked in the apartment we were going to. However, I still like carrot cake!

He brought us to an apartment that we were going to stay in. It was a one bedroom on the second floor. For beds, it had three twin mattresses set on box springs on the floor, and each bed had a pillow, some sheets and a few blankets. Each of us were given some soap, a tooth brush, tooth paste, a cup, a plate, a spoon, a knife and fork and three cooking pots for us to cook our food. That first evening we got to the apartment, I just went to bed, having had very little sleep, not feeling well, and completely overwhelmed. I remember it was the best sleep I ever had. When I woke up, guess what I had to eat? Carrot cake and orange juice! I go through the grocery store now and sometimes fill up two carts, I even know which brands are less expensive. I look back on that now remembering how clumsy we were at first.

The other women I was with were older than me, in their late twenties. They were of the same tribe as each other, and wouldn't you know it, I was from an opposite tribe that was fighting with theirs. Our tribe had beaten theirs during the civil war, and they were upset with me. They rejected me right away, when they found out and wouldn't have anything to do with me. It was very tense, very uncomfortable. They were very mean.

The social worker came by in the morning to take us to the Social Security office, where we did our paper work. From there we went to the social services agency to get $200 each in food stamps and a "Welcome to

America" cash amount of $150, which was a one time thing. When we got back to the apartment, I was dead sick again. I couldn't swallow, had a rash, my eyes were burning, and my throat was sore. For two days I lay in my bed, so sick I could barely get up to go to the bathroom.

That first day, two ladies brought some groceries - tea, and bread, fruit, chicken, and some canned goods, but the women I lived with didn't share with me. They would make their food and tea and then throw out what was left over, never offering me anything because of our tribal differences. I don't know which was worse, being sick to death or being ignored and humiliated by my roommates. They even called me derogatory names and bullied me. What a way to start my stay in America. It's not what I expected, however, I was used to the tribal differences issue which existed quite strongly in the refugee camp. There, we would avoid each other, but here, we had no choice. The social workers had no idea of tribes and clans and the trouble occurring in Somalia because of it.

Finally, after a few days, a very kind social worker came by. I remember it was a Tuesday. She asked my roommates where I was – "the third person?" They said, "Oh, she's in bed, we don't know what's wrong with her." The social worker came in and touched my forehead. Right away she said, "Come on, we're going to the hospital."

I crawled out of my bed, got my sandals, got dressed, and she held my arm and took me to the hospital in Phoenix. I was admitted there, where they gave me fluids, took blood from me, and gave me some IV medications. The social worker stayed with me the whole time; she was a wonderful woman; the first person, really, that I had any meaningful contact with. I wish I could see her again and thank her, but I don't know her name. I don't think I would have made it without her. It shows that with help, you can do anything. If she ever happens to read this book, I truly hope she contacts me, so that I can thank her.

I was in the hospital for a whole day and night and then went back to the apartment. The girls were even more malicious now. They'd make common jokes about me and how they hated my tribe. They'd say that I shouldn't even be in America – I didn't deserve it! I was used to insults and criticism, unfortunately. I didn't like it, but I guess I was able to take it from past experience.

One day, the three of us took a bus to go downtown. At one bus stop, they got off at the back of the bus and ditched me. The bus took off, and I had no idea where we were going or where to get off, as I couldn't read any English or any of the street signs, not even knowing where I was. I finally got off and sat on the bus bench not knowing what to do. Providentially, along came a Somali man and asked what I was doing. I told him what had happened, and that I had no idea where I was or how to get home. He told me there was only one bus that goes, and that I should take that and get off at a certain street. So I did it and found my way back to the apartment.

I was in the apartment with these women for about a month. Several Somali males would come by to visit us, as they heard there were some women living together, new to America, and they were looking for mates. One of them, Aden, visited often. He had a car and would help us by taking us to different places. He also helped us fill out job applications. It so happened that a friend of his worked at the Ritz Carlton hotel, so he helped two of us girls get jobs there. If it weren't for him and other immigrants, Somali as well as Mexican, that understood our predicament, we would have had a very difficult time. But, they showed us what we needed to do.

A real act of kindness shown to me, which I'll never forget, happened at the Ritz Carlton on my first day of work. I only had my one pair of sandals, which I brought with me from Somalia, so that's what I wore to work. The supervisor, Emilio, a very nice young Mexican man, told me I couldn't wear those at work, and that I needed regular shoes. I told him I didn't have any shoes and no money to buy some. So he went to his locker and brought me a pair of his shoes, they were black dress shoes. I was so impressed that a man was kind enough to actually give me his shoes. So I thanked him, and wore his shoes - every day until I could afford to buy my own. I wonder how many American girls would wear a pair of men's black dress shoes to work each day for a month or so - probably not too many! I thought it was great – nice pair of shoes!

For my first job at the Ritz Carlton, I started working as a dishwasher in the kitchen. At first, it was overwhelming; it was very hard getting used to the work schedule, starting at a certain time every day, breaks at another certain time, and ending at a certain time – with time clocks. Plus, that kind of work was new to me. The dishes just kept coming and coming, I had never used machines before like spraying water, running the dishes through the washer, and re-stacking them once they were cleaned.

The work and new life as a dishwasher, it was all like a blur to me. I didn't even know how to tell time - I learn quickly though. One of the guys at the Carlton liked me and taught me how to read the clock. I saw watches before, but never clocks on walls, where everyone watched them all day long. In the village we would tell time by the shadows cast from the sun. We could tell whether it was midday or not or time to start heading home as evening was approaching.

Looking back on my life in Somalia, sometimes it feels refreshing. Here you're aware of the clock all the time, go here, go there, punch in, punch out, lunch time, supper time, the clock says 10:00 at night so it must be time to go to bed, and so forth. In Somalia, we would not pay so much attention to the time. Sometimes the days were long, sometimes they were short. I think this is why some Americans have a problem with people coming here from Africa or a third world nation; but they need to understand, that we aren't programmed to watch a clock so closely. To us, 2:00 p.m. means a little while after the sun is highest in the sky, rather than, "Oh, my word, it's 1:45, and I have to get across town for my doctor's appointment. I'm going to be late."

I worked at the Carlton with many people from Mexico, and from them I learned how to speak Spanish and understand it fairly well. They spoke to me mainly in Spanish, not English, and before too long, I learned how to speak it. They were kind enough to not turn a cold shoulder to me, but to help me understand their language. So, the first language I learned in America was not English, but Spanish!

A difficult thing working for the hotel, was that we weren't allowed to wear a scarf or dresses - only pants and a blouse. What a shock! There were several Somali women that refused work because of this. I felt like I had no choice, and I had to do what I had to do – good lessons learned from Grandma and the village! What really helped me, was remembering my mother and siblings back in their tent in Dadaab, trying to barter for powdered milk or tea. So, I put on my pants and shirt, took the scarf off my head and went to work!

I felt like I was naked wearing the navy blue pants and my white shirt tucked in - and no scarf on my head! I remember, the first time I got my uniform, they asked me what size I wore, and I said, "I don't know; I told them I didn't know what size I was. What's a size?" I didn't even know what a size meant. I was very skinny at that time, so they found a uniform that would fit me. I know what size I am now, and I'd swap knowing that for being skinny again!

It only took me one month after I started working to begin sending money to my mother. Usually it was

$100, but sometimes as much as $300 per month – every month! I found out that many of the Somali immigrants to America work two jobs, one for themselves and their family and one for their relatives back in that war weary country. As time went on, I was able to send $800, so that my mother could rent a house in South Cea, a suburb of Nairobi. And, by continuing to send money, I helped her keep the house which she is still in to this day. I have also sent enough to put all my siblings through school, the youngest, little Mohamud being now a teenager and doing very well in school.

I worked at the Carlton for one year. I was well liked by most of my co-workers there, as I was a hard worker and always helped out when it was needed - without complaining. One time, I worked on a Saturday and the bus only ran until noon, yet I had to work until 3:30. I rode the bus to work, not even realizing there was no return bus, and it was a long walk back to my apartment. I wasn't comfortable walking home, because you could get hurt or raped or worse. Plus, my defense mechanisms kicked in from the grasslands of Somalia, and I knew better than to try that. One of my co-workers, a young Mexican man again, helped me. I had to wait until 8:00 that night when he got off work to get a ride, but I was glad to wait for him. I learned from one experience in Phoenix, when I was walking by myself when there was no bus. Two white guys stopped in their car and said really nasty things to me, fowl things that shouldn't even be said. It really scared me. So, I willingly waited from 3:30 until 8:00 that night for a ride home.

Working at the Carlton went well. After awhile I became more acquainted with people, and I was asked to work in the salad bar, pastry shop, and even help cook in the kitchen. They recognized that I was smart and learned quickly. I advanced well and was reliable, which helped to open doors for me, and, like I said, I was a quick learner.

One man, the chef named Michael, ended up being my friend and mentor. He advised me on how to be and how to act with guys that liked me - or pretended to like me! There was one young man in particular, that was very smooth with his talk and actions. He kept trying to be close with me. Michael told me not to go with him or to be alone with him. He said that he was trying to fool me; I'm glad I took his advice. People coming from other countries, especially third world countries, are very vulnerable, not understanding anything really.

After about a month of working at the Carlton, a Somali girlfriend of mine asked if I wanted to live with her and her two brothers. I had told her about the poor treatment from my roommates, and how I wished I could get away from them. She worked at the Sheraton hotel just down the street from where I worked, so I moved in with her. She and I shared a room, in fact, we shared a single bed – two girls sharing a single bed! But it worked, we slept, and we became good friends. Later, she got married, so I had to move again, as I did not want to live with her brothers by myself – my memories of my nomad days were way too fresh in my mind, and that was never going to happen to me again. So, I moved in with a lady from work; it was her and husband, their son and her sister. They were very nice to me and welcomed me into their home.

America was all new to me. There was food everywhere, especially at the Ritz Carlton – cookies, sweets, pastries, small little sandwiches, large buffets served to lots of people, and I was able to eat there for free. I went from porridge and milk to more food than I have ever seen before. Pizza was the most amazing thing I had ever seen or tasted; I was mesmerized by it! McDonald's just blew my mind; when I went to McDonalds, it was that very day that I fell in love with America. Slowly, slowly, I was getting used to the culture here.

I was uncomfortable, however, by the affection shown between the sexes. In Somalia what happens in the dark, stays in the dark. But here, everyone is touching everyone, kissing in public, affectionate; we aren't like that. My first time at the Social Security office, there were two people kissing right there in the lobby; I was shocked and embarrassed. To this day, I don't do that with my husband in public.

Being in Phoenix was kind of like being in a fog; everything was new to me, everything there was for the first time – a lot to absorb and process. There I went to the doctor for the first time with allergies and a rash. Here was an older man and said to me, "Oh I'm going to give you medicine and help you and make you feel better." He talked to me like I was his granddaughter. I thought, "Why is he being so nice?"

Everyone in America is very nice, very soft spoken. I realized OK, I am safe here. I hadn't felt that safe for a long time. In the camp, I was afraid of being raped and molested or robbed and killed. I became pretty trusting here in America, losing much of my fear.

I had to learn to drive, which was difficult. I'm very surprised I didn't kill someone with my driving. I'm so embarrassed now looking back on it. I also had to learn English, of course, so I went to "English as a second language" class - and failed it! After one year, however, I could hold my own. But, I still don't know how to read a map. I shopped in Phoenix and could find skirts and blouses. And, I learned American money. For a long time I would pay for something and give a lot more money than it cost – everything in my wallet! But the people were kind enough to give most of it back to me, except for what it really cost. I had to manage my own checking account, which proved interesting – buying things without money! I did worry, however, about what would happen if something happened to me; who would be there to help me? I was alone in America!

While all this was going on, I was calling and writing to a cousin of mine who lived in Minneapolis. A friend of hers, who she was living with, was going to get married and move out. So, my cousin invited me to move up to Minneapolis and stay with her in her apartment. I thought, "Why not?" So, I gave two weeks notice at the Carlton telling them I was going to quit – just like that.

Shortly before my last day, an odd thing happened to me. A famous guest came to stay at the Carlton, a black man, and he found out that there were Somali refugees working in the kitchen. He had the management bring him back there to us. I was working, and saw there was a lot of fuss over this man, and realized he must have been someone important. So, he came in and greeted us, hugged several of us including myself and asked to have his picture taken with me. Why me, I don't know, but I guess we connected. So I did. I had no idea who this man was. After the picture was taken, and the man left, I asked, "Who was that?" The Mexican guys in the kitchen broke out laughing, they said, "You silly girl, that was Mohammed Ali!"

I had been saving up money from working at the Carlton by not spending on anything frivolous or unnecessary, living mainly on peanut butter and jelly sandwiches. So, by the time I was ready to leave for Minneapolis, I had about $2400 saved up. I bought a plane ticket to Minneapolis, told my cousin I was coming, and off I went.

Chapter Fifteen

Life Smiles on Me

———•··•———

I'm very, very glad I didn't come to a snow area first thing, when I came to America. Phoenix was more like what I was used to in Somalia, and Kenya, hot and dry, and I didn't have a lot to get used to with regards to the weather and climate. However, why didn't anyone tell me about Minnesota? My first winter was terrible; I had never seen snow before much less mountains of it with freezing, driving winds that take your breath away, freeze your face and almost knock you off your feet. And driving in it, forget it! Now that was an adjustment for me. I would not be surprised if you saw some Somalis, especially ladies, wearing sandals when it's in the single digits outside, because we are not used to wearing tennis shoes, much less boots.

My cousin, who asked me to move to MN, forgot to mention she was not living alone, and that she did not have her own apartment. She was living with her friend, the friend's husband and their daughter in a two bedroom apartment. My cousin, the little girl and

I shared a bedroom, while the married couple slept in the other room. There were two twin beds in our room; the little girl slept in one, while my cousin and I slept in the other. I had to remind myself, that this was not as bad as when I used to sleep on the ground and tie cloths around my feet to keep the worms from burrowing in, or a rope around my legs so as not to get raped. After that, sleeping in a twin bed with a cousin would be what heaven is like - we each had a pillow, and the sheets and blankets were clean. Just as earlier settlers that came to America in the old days from the European countries, and now those from Africa, Asia, Mexico and other countries as well, many are doubling up living together, trying to get established and up on their feet. If it weren't for my own people and other immigrants helping me, I'm not sure I would have made it.

Living in Minneapolis, I soon found work, and actually, had two jobs. Both of them were as a cashier, one in a department store, and the other in a gift shop. I also learned how to get around in Minneapolis and figured out the bus system.

As words travel around very fast, especially in the immigrants' community, there was talk that a young girl had arrived in town. Who might that be? I guess me. The phone calls started to come in wanting to know who I was, and if I was willing to mingle and get married. So one day, when I was home from work, the phone rang. It was a young Somali man. He told me that he heard from a friend that I was new in town, and he wanted to know if he could take me out for coffee.

I was reluctant at first, not having met this man, but I said yes, anyway.

He came over to the apartment and introduced himself, saying his name was Abdi. We went to a coffee shop, sat there and conversed for a while, then he brought me back home. We had a nice time, I liked him. After that, we talked quite often on the phone. He was interested in getting married, but I was not really ready for that. He was very persistent, so to get him of my back, I said if you are really serious, call my dad and uncle. In our culture, the man must talk to the girl's parents and get the approval from them. I thought he was not going to do it, maybe chicken out, but he didn't. Within three months, we got married. When I was back in the village, dreaming about my own husband and hut, I had no idea it would be in Minneapolis, Minnesota. I didn't really know what I was getting into, though, because the idea of getting married and being actually married is completely different. I would not want my daughters, or even son, to get married at a young age.

Being a young, healthy Somali woman, I got pregnant right away with my oldest daughter – Najma. I worked through my pregnancy which went very well, although I was tired and had a sore back all the time. What I wasn't prepared for, though, was being a mother. I had no education in this area, not even from my own mother or grandmother. So, I had no idea what to do with a baby. I breast fed her, but when she got constipated or sick or had ear aches, I didn't know how to care for her. I was afraid to take her to the doctor, as I thought the medicines she would be given would kill her. So, I did the best I could to be a nurse to her, as well as a mother. Honestly, many times I thought back to taking care of the baby sheep and goats, many of which had their little illnesses. Somehow, Najma survived my nursing, and today is a beautiful, intelligent, young girl making her way through school.

I immediately fell into the role that is expected of a married Somali woman. I spent most of my time at home with Najma, rarely going out of the apartment we were renting. I would just wait for Abdi to come home from work at night to have someone to talk to – sound familiar, girls? Well, it wasn't familiar to me, and I didn't know how to handle it. I spent many, many days in my bedroom crying, all alone. Finally, a friend of ours suggested that I go to school to be a nursing assistant. This sounded good to me, and, after all, I took care of the goats and sheep, didn't I? I could certainly take care of patients!

I went to the Community College that taught nursing assistant courses, and they first had me take an assessment test to see where I stood as far as my math and English. Well, it didn't take long for them to see where I was at – I failed! I was devastated, I thought I'd never be able to do any more than just stay at home in the apartment and have babies. Well, as in many cases in my life, when I ran up against a brick wall, I took the challenge and decided, "No, I'm going to do this." So, I went to the library, got tapes and books on English and math and studied, and studied, and studied.

I went back to the College about six weeks later, took the assessment test, and barely made it. But I made it, and that's all that mattered.

I got my first job in a nursing home taking care of mainly elderly white people. I really enjoyed it. I liked the old folks. But, this was the first time in my life I had to deal with racism directed at me. Some of the old people would make comments to me about my color or how I dressed, but I realized they didn't know any better and probably had never seen anyone look like me before. I remembered how we treated the Bantu – just because their ancestors came from a different part of the world. We never would marry them, associate with them, or invite them into our homes. Now I learned what it felt like, and I'm glad I did, as it taught me a lesson.

I worked for the nursing home for three years. I really enjoyed working there, and, for the most part, they liked me as well. I was a hard worker, always willing to do what I was asked, and got along with everyone. While working there, I continued to learn English and math. I had a good friend who was a college student, and she would come by and tutor me once per week to help me. I really got to like Hawthorne as a writer, I thought he was great – still do!

After several years of working, I decided I couldn't be a nursing assistant forever, because I needed more money for my family. Abdi did well making a living for us, but I remembered what I thought about America, that it was wealthy and its people could be wealthy as well. What I had to learn, however, was that you have to work for it! So, I launched on my endeavor to become a nurse. I decided to first become an LPN to improve my working situation and my salary, and then I would go on to become an RN. I took all my prerequisites like anatomy and chemistry, math and English and had a 4.0 grade point average. When I was applying to the LPN program at the community college, my school friends said, "Oh Habibo, you will not survive this school. They are so tough and racist. They will make you fail."

I told them, "If my hard work and good attitude does not get me through this school, then I have worked for nothing. I have good work ethics and dedication, I have never backed out of a challenge and I'm not going to quit now." To my surprise, I was accepted into the LPN program. I was so excited. I couldn't believe I was accepted.

At first, the other students and teachers treated me like I was definitely a second class citizen. They shied away from me, and I even had teachers say to me, "Habibo, nursing is going to be too hard for you. Why don't you think about doing something else? You're more suited to wash dishes or clean houses." This kind of talk only fuels my determination. Those students and teachers didn't know it, but they did me a favor, as I set my mind to accomplishing this task, and I was going to do it.

Well, after the first term, I maintained my 4.0 grade point average. Immediately, all the poor treatment and snide remarks and put downs stopped. I even had students asking to study with me, and teachers treating me very well and with respect. Is there a lesson here? It's sad that one has to be really great in order to be liked. What about those that don't do so well?

We students developed a study group to help each other learn nursing. We had a lady in the group who was gay. This was my first exposure to this, as being gay would mean death for anyone in Somalia, so you never knew who was gay! At first I didn't know what to think, but I was OK with it. She was very nice, intelligent, kind and actually became a good friend of mine.

When we all graduated from nurse's training, I'll never forget the instructor that I thought was the most difficult and hard to get along with. She gave the speech for the graduating class, and she said, "There is one student who was the most quiet, the most dedicated and the most likely to succeed – Habibo! I was shocked; I didn't know what to think, but I was very happy for the praise, as I worked hard to do a good job.

During all this, Abdi was working in Rochester, Minnesota, about a one hour drive south of the Twin Cities. We decided to move there to make life easier for Abdi, and I knew that being a nurse, I could find work there. What I didn't know, was that I would find it at a very prestigious place – the Mayo Clinic – where I work to this day.

I'll never forget my interview there. I applied for a nursing job and didn't hear anything for quite some time, maybe a month or so. Finally, I got called and was asked to come in for an interview. I was an absolute wreck. I thought, "How can I do this? I'm not smart enough to do this." But, I remembered my uncle, Ahmed, saying the very same thing when I lost one of our sheep, and he had to jump into the river with crocodiles to save it. He also said, "How can I do this?" Well, I saw what he went through making that decision. He was tormented and frustrated and afraid, but he jumped in and saved the sheep. Have you ever gone to an interview feeling like you were jumping into a river of crocodiles? I imagine you have.

The interview went well. To make a long story short, I continued my studies to transition to a registered nurse while working at Mayo. Now that I'm an RN, I'm taking courses to complete my BS in nursing. After which, now that I know I can do it, I'll proceed to my Masters degree. Some people ask me, "Why, Habibo? Why continue on so far, so hard. You have a good job and a nice house now." My answer is always, "Because I can!" But above all, I want to show my girls and other girls around the world, that anything is possible with determination and patience.

Chapter Sixteen

From Here on In

Many people from Somalia are now living in various parts of the world, while our home country is still trying to keep itself from self-destructing. Being that we are living in other cultures, we are losing the values we grew up with and not adapting well enough to the new cultures we're in.

For example, the other day I was taking the bus after I got off work and, as usual, the bus was very full. There were two young Somali men, probably about twenty years of age that were riding the bus as well. They had to stand along with about six others with no seats available. One elderly lady, maybe in her late 70s, was also standing trying to keep her balance, along with these two young men who had no trouble keeping their balance. Some people got out of the bus, and a few seats became available; those two young men had the audacity to sit down on the two remaining seats, before the elderly lady could sit down. I have never been more disappointed and embarrassed in my life before that day. Back home, growing up in the village, we had respect for our elderly. We never sat down anywhere, while an older person was standing.

I asked those two young men why did they not give up the seat for the elderly lady? One of them said, "Why would I do that? I need to sit as well, and who cares about the old lady anyway?"

So I asked if his parents would be disappointed in him. He said, "I don't care what they think of me." I then asked him what he sees himself doing in five years.

He said, "I don't think that far ahead. I'm just having fun now."

What a shame, what a sad picture. This is one of the reasons I want to write my story, and see if somehow I could make a difference here in the USA as well as back home. The kids here need lots of guidance and social supports, whereas back in the village, kids need schools and educational materials.

Somalia, having no government in over twenty years and riddled with tribal warfare, is just now starting to turn itself around. A president has been elected along with a parliament. However, much fighting continues outside of the capital of Mogadishu. Everyone there is still on their own, many tribes controlling many areas. There are breakouts and fights and people getting killed for no reason, with a lot of younger kids with no way of occupying themselves, except carrying a gun and killing - so very sad! I recently received a call from my aunt in Somalia, who said her son, 15 years old, was injured from a gunshot.

I call my mother usually once per week, or she'll call me. Whenever I talk to her or some relative, there's always news that someone died recently, or someone got killed. Just recently, I received a voice mail from a younger cousin of mine, telling me that my uncle's son was riding a bike, when he and about twenty other people were killed by a bomb. How sad!

The poverty level is really bad - no jobs, hunger, younger children suffering, no way of getting aid and supplies to the country, because it's not a safe place. Many young people in Somalia have nothing to do, so guns are their toys, and for $100 they'll shoot someone for you. My cousin was shot two years ago for $200. These kids were born during this whole turmoil, so all they know is fighting. I have high hopes for my country to get back to normal and become safe for all people. I also have hope that the spirit of tribalism will decrease, and that tribes and clans will get along for the sake of the country and its people. We need strong, determined, unselfish people to run the country. We, as a community, need to realize that life is precious, our childrens' future matters, and we need to make the country and the world a better place.

Because of the trouble in my home country, Dadaab refugee camp has now swollen to one half of a million people. I have never been back there since I left, but I just can't imagine what it's like being that extremely large. I understand it has hospitals now, schools, and stores just like a city – a city of tents. Unfortunately, all one half million have nothing to do – no work, no animals to graze, no crops to tend, nothing! I plan to return to Dadaab to see it for myself.

From the time I moved my mother and siblings out of Dadaab, they have lived in Nairobi. The kids have been able to go to school there, and are doing very well. I missed my mom and my siblings more than anything, and not seeing them for twelve years was extremely hard.

When I first came to the United States back in 1999, I was able to file sponsorship for my mother and my siblings. I worked very hard to bring them here, but it didn't work out the way I was hoping for. When I first filed the papers, my mother got a letter a year after stating she would be contacted for a formal interview. It took two more years before she got that interview. She and the rest of the family had to go through a primary interview, secondary interview, and were finally told they passed all the processing and could expect their orientation times within the next few months. They had their orientation, which is basically telling you most things you need to know before you enter the United States. They completed that in May of 2003. I was SO excited, and was hoping that they would come before the birth of my second daughter who was due later that year.

I got a call from the office of the Catholic Charities to sign the acceptance forms for the family, which states that I would provide for them the first six months that they are here. Again, I was ecstatic to sign this paper, knowing that in a few weeks to a month, I would see my family again. We waited and waited anxiously, and the weeks turned into months and months into years. During this waiting period my mother and I had been writing and calling to find out what was the hold up, and if there was anything we could do to speed up the process. During that period, my hopes and dreams of reuniting with my family were shattered, and I became sad, depressed and gave up all hopes of them coming to the US.

My family had three medical checkups, six different interviews, two orientations, a DNA test, but ultimately, in November of 2009, they were told that they were not accepted to the United States. That is ten years of waiting and hoping; ten years that our lives were on hold. Sometimes I used to think those people do not have hearts, because as a human being how can you do that to people - make them wait for ten years then tell them, "Sorry we cannot accept you." It would be better if they had told us from the beginning, so that my family and I could move on with our lives, so that we could plan to reunite in some other way.

In early 2010, when I finally realized that my family was not going to come to the United States, I made the decision to go and visit them in Kenya. This was not an easy decision, mainly due to the cost. However, my mother had not seen any of my kids, and more than anything, she wanted to see her only grandchildren. When I called my mother to tell her that I was going to come visit them, my mother's first reaction was, "Oh! Good! I'm finally going to see my grandkids."

I told her, "I'm sorry to disappoint you Mom, but I can't bring the kids due to the cost."

Needless to say, she was very disappointed. It was very hard not being able to take my kids with me, so that they could see my family, but that was almost impossible. So when I left, I kissed my children good bye, got on the plane and headed back to Africa.

The plane landed in Nairobi early in the morning. And, of course, no one was there to meet me. Why this always happens to me, I don't know, but I'm getting used to it. Rather than panicking, I simply waited, knowing someone, sometime would show up to pick me up. I decided to have some coffee, so I sat with a man in the coffee shop who was from Washington, DC. We had a good conversation, and I thought how odd it was that only a dozen years after I left Dadaab, barely old enough to be called an adult, not knowing any English, very uncultured and rather ignorant about the world, here I was sitting and conversing about American politics with a man from the nation's capital.

As we were talking, I looked up and there, before my eyes walking towards me, was my uncle, Ahmed, and next to him my mother. Ahmed, in his long flowing robe looked so stately, although he looked older and thinner with gray hair now. But his eyes, his eyes still were soft and gentle, very caring. My mother also showed the years on her face, now having six children to take care of - and all in their teenage years.

I jumped up and ran toward them. I first ran to my mother and hugged her for what seemed like forever, not wanting to let go; than I hugged Uncle Ahmed, and we all started to cry with joy. And Ahmed, of all people! I couldn't have wished for anyone else in the world to come there to greet me. They kept commenting on how I became such a grown woman.

Ahmed said, "Habibo, the last time I saw you, you were a little girl, barely more than sixteen; now you are a woman and a beautiful one at that."

I enjoyed my stay with my mother. It was really nice not having to get up at 5:30 every morning to go to work. I spent a great deal of time with my and my siblings. Sometimes we stayed up until 3:00 a.m. talking about random stuff. The girls and I went out a couple of times and got our hair, nails, and facials done. It was so nice to get to know them. They barely remembered me from when I left. I was also able to see that all the hard work I had put in to help them financially, was not a waste as their education level is very good now.

Ahmed came over every day for lunch. We talked about many things, remembering the time I went away with the cows for several months, and the time he fell from the tree, and also when he had to swim in the river to save the sheep. We reminisced about planting the barley and the many long talks we had.

I spent sixteen days there with them in Nairobi. We did all the family things that people do: we slept and ate, shopped, visited a lot, and I spent much time playing with the kids getting to know them, and letting them get to know me. I had so much fun going out and buying them things, like new clothes and shoes, little things that they couldn't afford. I think my mother recognized me now as a grown woman, wiser than when I left. She never did show a whole lot of affection, which is her way, similar to my grandmother, but I could tell she was impressed with how I had changed and matured.

It was odd being back in Africa. Not much was different. The main thing that changed since I was back there before, was me! I had become Westernized, I realized. Nairobi, which in my eyes was a large bustling city with large buildings and some running water, now looked like a third world city to me. The majority of roads were still dirt, nothing like the tar and cement roads in America, not even as nice as the gravel roads you find in the American countryside. Sidewalks? Not in Nairobi. Our clothes got dirty from walking in the dirt streets, many of which were muddy and crowded, with people everywhere.

The buses which ran were not as dependable as in the States. When I ride the bus going to work at Mayo, I get on, show my card and walk back to a seat. When you get onto a bus in Nairobi, you barely put your foot in the door, and the driver guns it and you're off. We ate out a lot while I was there, but I was always concerned about bacteria. Being a nurse, I'm always concerned about that, but in Nairobi, one has to be very concerned. Cleanliness, storage of food, hand washing practices, many times are quite lacking.

My mother's apartment, which I helped to pay for several years before, was kind of a shock to me. It was in an older building, somewhat crumbling and not very well kept. They lived on the first floor which seemed to get dirty quite easy. Most of the apartments there have running water, but not hot water. Toilets are inside, but if the water all of a sudden is turned off, then it's impossible to flush. And, sometimes the water is off for several days to a week.

I told my mother, "Mom, I'm getting you out of here. I think we can find something much nicer for you."

So, we looked around and found a nice apartment on the third floor of a different building. I paid for it for her and helped her and the kids move into it. When I left there, I felt much better knowing that they were in good living conditions – safer, cleaner, and with more space.

Remembering the last time I saw my mother and siblings, living in a makeshift tent on the edge of Dadaab refugee camp, it was a proud moment for me to see them living more civilized with beds and sheets, towels and several sets of clothes. It made me feel good that I was able to help them have that. I could see that my efforts immigrating to the United States, and working as hard as I did for quite a few years, had its rewards, not only for myself, but for them as well. It affirmed that what I was doing was worthwhile.

The time came for me to leave. It was sad saying goodbye to my mother and siblings again, but when it came time to go, it was time to go; I had my own family to return to that needed me also. The long plane rides from Nairobi to Amsterdam, then on to New York and Minnesota gave me plenty of time to absorb what I'd seen in Africa. I realized I had become more mature in my thinking, and rather than feeling like I just didn't match up, or was somewhat "less than" others, I now began to think, "Hey, I did the best I could. I'm OK."

I look back now at everything that happened in my past, from being a toddler in my grandmother's hut by myself eating a little porridge and playing with mud, to the times my cousin would visit the hut or when I stayed with them, to all the times I went out with the animals into the grasslands. I thought about how rugged a person would have to be in order to do that, to work each day walking sheep and goats and cows miles and miles so they could eat, and then fighting off the wild animals trying to eat the herd. I remembered the crocodile that looked into my eyes – I'll never forget his! Trust me, you don't want to experience that. I thought about the times I was taken advantage of as a young girl and through my growing up years, until I went to Dadaab, when it finally stopped, and I didn't have to fight anymore.

I looked out the plane window, as we were flying over the Atlantic. Here I was, dressed nice, carrying a purse with money and charge cards, a U.S. citizen with a driver's license and being a Registered Nurse, flying home to my nice job at the Mayo Clinic and my nice house with a large screen TV, nice furniture, king size bed with lots of pillows, and my children! I thought to myself, "What a life! How did I get here?"

I'm still processing some of what I went through in my life, especially the very difficult times. Surprisingly enough, it's not so much the times I had to fight the camel boys off or being treated badly from my fifteen year old cousin, it's the criticism and belittlement, and the lack of support and care that I had to endure growing up as a young girl. The feeling of not really being wanted, being more of a farm hand and not belonging to anyone, that's the hard part! I didn't have hugs and kisses, people telling me they loved me, praise of any kind. Being alone was hard!

I realize now that I wasn't the only one going through that. Thousands and thousands all over the world go through it, and not just in third world countries. Right here in America, I see it all around me in the faces and eyes of young girls and boys, as well as adults.

I'm sharing my story with you, because it's so very common to many people, especially many young girls around the world. Those girls who still live in my village, those young men and women that are still nomads who have never set a foot in schools, who are not aware of their brilliant talents, who have never been told they are worth more than just bearing children. And, for those girls and boys who were born in Dadaab and still being born in Dadaab, who have no hope of getting out of there and, most importantly, no hope whatsoever for an education. I'm writing this for anyone whose innocence has been stolen as a child, for anyone who has been told they were not good enough, or pretty enough or anyone who ever felt left out or unloved. This is for you.

When a child is born, they are innocent and deserve the absolute best life can provide. Parents are responsible for providing this, which means providing that child with support: financial, educational, spiritual, emotional, intellectual, and an overall sense of well-being. One of the most important things I found out in my life, is that a child needs to know he or she is being loved by his or her parents, unconditionally. That a parent's love cannot be bought or denied, and that is something the child is entitled to and not something that needs to be earned. With love and appreciation, children can develop a sense of belonging and can grow up to become self-sufficient, independent, successful individuals who can contribute to society. No child should ever feel unloved or unworthy of love.

I'm sharing my story, because I want to make a difference, I want to advocate for young girls who have no opportunity for education. With education, we can eradicate ignorance. There are millions of children that have no access to schools in sub-Sahara Africa or Asia. Of those children, eighty percent are girls.

Sharing my story is one of the most difficult things I've had to do in my life, because it required that I revisit, or remember, certain aspects of my life that I buried a long time ago. I realize, in spite of the difficulty, I've been very, very fortunate. God had plans for me, and still does. My faith has grown much stronger as I see how life can turn out, and how sometimes life throws us good things as well as bad. From each, we learn.

People ask me, "Oh, Habibo, how were you able to do what you did?"

I say, "Plain and simple - sheer determination to survive, to improve, and to make a better life for myself and those around me."

I especially try to be for my children, what no one was for me. My attitude with them is not one of criticism – ever! When they try to do things and fail, I say, "Don't worry about it, you'll get it next time."

However, I do not spoil my children, either. Even though I didn't have anything – no toys, one pair of tire sandals, one dress, maybe two in good years, sleeping in the dirt most of the time - I tell my children that many people do not get the opportunities they get, many of which they need to work for and earn. I tell them to appreciate what they have, and I remind them of how I grew up.

As a parent I try to do the best I can, and as I get older I realize new things every day. I know that I'm far from perfect, and make my own mistakes with my children. I decide when my girls and young son get to watch TV, and what kind of TV they watch. Many times they don't want to do the things they're supposed to, like their homework, or their cleaning jobs, or meeting with their tutor. I tell them, "What you have is a privilege. You have TV and a cell phone and nice clothes and a tutor, because you've earned it, you're worth it. But with it comes a price, you have to do your part as well." Am I always successful, no! But, you know what? I do the best I can!

I want to make a difference through sharing me story, educating parents and kids, through speaking, my website and hopefully opening a foundation soon that supports young girls and boys who would otherwise not have an opportunity to get an education. I strongly believe we can make a difference through education, and making parents aware of the importance of education. I would also strongly advocate for discontinuation of female circumcision, because it has no basis in our religion and science.

Thank you for letting me share my story with you. It's one of many, many stories. I hope it was of benefit to you and pray that God will bless your lives. Since the start of writing it, my husband and I have parted ways. I pray that God blesses his life as well.

The End
Or Perhaps the Beginning

Epilogue

Clans – what's it all about?

Somali is like saying Caucasian, but it has many tribes within it with many generations and descendents. Within Caucasian is English, Irish, Spanish, German, French and so on, so it is with Somali. There is a book by the former transition President that states education is one of the keys to getting the country back. However, it can take years. I was aware of tribes growing up in the village. I knew who I was and what tribe I was in, not out of animosity with other tribes, but just that I belonged to a certain tribe and clan. Growing up I didn't hear much about tribalism. When the war was happening, yes, we became afraid of other tribes, but growing up I was not so aware of it. The area I grew up in was one big parent tribe. Being a part of this tribe bound you together to fight outside tribes.

I didn't know about other country's involvement in Somalia, until I was in America and studied more about Somali history. I'm surprised no other countries really said, "Let's help these guys out since we had a history there," such as England, Italy, Russia, and America. I believe they have an obligation to not let people kill each other yet they do nothing about it. They were there because it's a very rich country with many resources, large tracts of land along the ocean and not to mention the Gulf of Aden.

I hope that my kids can go back some day. The Somali children here in America are caught between cultures. There are two groups of Somali here – the elderly and the young kids. The young ones need help the most. I want to travel to third world countries as a nurse, but now my responsibility is being a mother, but when my kids grow older I can do it.

In any situation and any country you should give kids the right tools, tell them your expectations and what's acceptable. If they can't do that, then you have to give them a reason such as no alcohol, smoking, no pants on the ground. Why not take the culture that has more opportunity than the one that doesn't?

Summertime in America, young kids can get involved in community activities, soccer, softball, camping – many Somali don't know they can do that, so they don't sign their kids up. So when both parents work, the kids run crazy and get into trouble. They need parent's involvement as little humans. In the village all watched after all kids, parents were not the only guiders, so even to sneak and get into trouble other adults would scold you. Here, there's nothing like that.

༄

Is there a reason for your life?

There is a purpose for all people's lives, some will tell you it's to worship others would say it's having strong faith. The bigger picture is that the sky's the limit - I'm the one that can make it or not. I was recently thinking I want a PhD and get into community involvement with those from my culture. There is a great need for someone to guide them: they especially the elderlies don't know their medications, they don't understand their diseases, and they don't know how to fit into American culture; they don't know the system.

For me, the bigger picture is educating people to better themselves. I want to educate people. When I'm fifty six, and if I'm still living, I hope to be educating people and doing community work – giving back to the world from what it gave to me.

༄

What did the village teach you about life?

It taught me to be resilient and hard working, not to give up easily. It forced me to grow up sooner. I learned how to rely on myself. I had to chase hyenas and jackals and crocodiles with nothing but a stick; it taught me to be strong. I'm able to do things for myself and my family, and I don't have to rely on someone to do it for me. Sometimes this is not the best approach though, because it creative frictions in my relationships, because I can be hard headed and think that it's me against the world.

However, I can take this to an extreme. My family and friends are always telling me – you don't have to act like you're on your own in this world, thinking you have to do it all, it's ok to let someone else help. It's hard for me to do that. It's not good to have things done your way or in your time. Sometimes you have to let it slide, and let someone else take their time. I run into trouble when I have to do it now and get it done. I'm learning to let it go, that it's not the end of the world.

☙

You didn't mention anything about female circumcision. Did that go on in your village?

Yes, it went on in our village and every village and city in Somalia. Somalia has been described by anthropologists as "the land of sewn women," with millions of women having undergone this procedure for hundreds of years. However, in my opinion, "procedure" or "surgery" are words that are too civilized for what really happens. In fact, mutilation is a more accurate term.

Each year in mid-summer between planting and harvesting, all the young girls between the ages of seven and nine are gathered together for their circumcision; sometimes called pharaonic circumcision after the pharaoh who, thousands of years ago started it. He started it when he went on a long journey, and did not want his wife cheating on him. So, he had her genital area sewn together except for a small opening to urinate. This is how girls grow up from seven or so until they are married. At which time, her husband "opens" her genitals on their wedding night. Sound like fun?

An older woman in our village, and several other women, would gather together at a central area with a few "common" huts which were used for various community type events. Any young girl that needed the procedure done would be brought to them. I remember each year hearing it happen, as the screams would sound through the whole village. Those screams I can't get out of my head; I can still hear them if I close my eyes. The young girls would wait in line outside one of the "common" huts, waiting for their turn under the razor, waiting for two of the older women to come out and take them inside. It was so scary and so awful, yet because of peer pressure and not wanting to be "different" than the other girls and women, everyone complied. It happened every year, year after year, for all females in the country – and still does!

The girls would stand in line waiting their turn, and while standing there, they could hear the girl ahead of them, inside the hut, screaming and struggling. She could be heard throughout the village, as there was nothing to deaden the pain, no anesthesia, not even sterile instruments. When the screaming stopped, it wasn't too long before she was carried out of the hut by two of the women, her legs tied together, blood covering her legs and dress, and a far-away look in her eyes. They'd place her out under a tree with the other girls that went ahead of her, and there they'd wait until it was all over, when they would all enjoy, or try to enjoy, a little celebration with food and drinks.

After carrying her out, they came for the next girl in line, usually frozen with fear and extremely reluctant to go inside. Soon, the screaming and crying and pleading to stop would begin again, but the old woman would not stop until the job was done.

Inside the hut, on the ground on a wooden bed like a pallet, was a cloth thrown over the large bloody area from the girl before. Under it was another cloth that lay beneath the last girl, and under it a cloth from the girl before that. And so, the cloths just built up to soak up as much blood as they could, until the last girl was taken care of. Blood dripped off the pallet; in a wooden bowl lay the bloody tissue that was removed.

After the old woman finished, she stitched the girl's labia together using a thorn and small, very thin, pieces of cloth. She took a opening where urine could be released; while stitching, a stick was placed at the opening of the girl's urethra to make sure it wasn't sewn shut accidentally. The skin was to grow together except for this one small opening. It was to stay this way until the girl's wedding night when her husband would reopen it by force. If her husband was not able to open it during his attempts at intercourse, then he was labeled as "weak."

It would take about four to six weeks for the girl to heal, during which time she would lay in her family's hut on her wooden cot, legs still tied together, urinating, relieving herself right 0there to be cleaned up by the women of the family. In order to minimize the need to urinate or defecate, no food and only sips of water or milk are given for that whole time.

After the two weeks was up, the girls are taken back to the old woman's hut to be inspected. Like many girls before, if everything wasn't looking the way it should, then the procedure would be repeated.

ॐ

What about the boys?

The same thing, only easier. At about seven or eight years old, boys were taken to the "common" area, held down, and with a knife, the same knife for all of them, their foreskin was removed. End of story.

ॐ

Do you regret your life up to the time when you came to America?

No regrets. I wouldn't be who I am today, if I had a different life. At times, I wish I had it easier, better than what I did. But more than anything, I wish I had my father in my live growing up. I could've been poor, but if I had two parents who loved me and showed concerns for my wellbeing and safety, life would have been so much different. I couldn't have made it this far, if I hadn't gone through it. Being humble – I see someone going through problems and tough times, I'm humbled in that I can empathize with them. I don't talk about their misery, or criticize and I don't gossip. We nurses are in a position to take care of people, not to put them down or criticize. Their life is not our life; we haven't gone through what they went through. You're given the privilege to treat them, and you have to respect that.

Because of the way I was raised, I have a lack of relating to others, and it's hard to develop close personal relationships. I tend to be closed off, a loner, and only see things my way, stubborn. I can make friends, but establishing a deep connection and completely trusting someone? I'm afraid of getting hurt and am troubled by self doubt. I often have to take a deep breath. I learned there are some things I can change; I don't have to cut myself off the first time I'm disappointed. I can forgive or learn to forgive. I'm a work in progress. I've learned to take one day at a time, and if something bothers me, I take a deep breath and ask myself, is it really so important that I'm stressing out over it? If it's life and death or absolutely something I have to deal with, I'll act on it. But, if it won't change or it's minor, I let it fly. My therapist and I have discussed this issue of being "closed off" she states because I had experienced abandonment as a child it's in my nature to revert back to those feeling the minute I think I might get hurt in a situations. She made me realize why I had hard time forming meaningful friendships all these years.

෨

What do you miss the most about Somalia?

My village! I absolutely envision going back someday, especially when it rains and there's green everywhere. I'd like to walk to all my little favorite spots by the river. There's a huge tree in the village which you could climb and see a long ways out for miles. I believe it's called a qansah tree. I'd like to climb that tree one more time. I miss the farm when the barley was tall enough to hide in it. My favorite thing to do when I had some free time was to run and scream in it. It felt amazing with the smells taking you away. I miss late at night when you can hear the hyenas howl, and the morning when the birds wake up from sleeping in the trees then making circles around the barley fields diving and dipping. My cows I miss. They were my favorite, so big, so gentle; when full they'd lie down and I'd sleep with them, rub them. They treated me good, my favorites.

❧

What do you think about American culture?

Great stuff - hamburgers, McDonalds, the best meal I ever tasted was when I had my first Big Mac and fries. I thought, "Oh my word, this is fantastic!" America is fabulous with all the differences within it; it's amazing with its many diverse cultures, ethnicities, and religions side by side - that's what makes America what it is. If you just had one ethnicity, it wouldn't be America. There are negatives, but the good outweighs the bad. I'm glad there are laws in place to keep it safe; they help make it a better country. I like it that no one can discriminate based on gender, color, or orientation. I don't' watch the presidential or other elections, as I don't like negativity and making up bad information about people or saying bad things because you want to get ahead. If you're really good, people will see it; you don't have to make someone look bad to make you look good. People will see through it.

❧

Do you wish you would've grown up in a city, like Mogadishu?

I wish I would've grown up in a household where show affections and praise was shared, and shown, on a daily basis and a community where an education was available to all kids. Mogadishu was and is the capital of Somali, so of course people were more modernized than in my little village. To a child, it doesn't matter country or place, rich or poor, as long as he or she has good support system.

❧

What did you learn from all the many miles of walking and herding the animals?

I used to climb trees to get leaves when it was so dry out and very little for the cows to eat. I'd get big leaves from the tops of the trees to feed them; I'd drop them down and they'd stand underneath and eat. That felt good to be able to provide for them. Or, I'd swim to the opposite side of the river and get the long grass for them. I'd like to do that once more - but only once. I'd like to just take the day with the cows, go swimming before coming home at night. I've never had the chance to be by myself since then. When I was out herding, I was with myself most of the time, but I was never alone. I'd talk with the animals, the cows. I'd play with them and be involved in their day. I felt so comfortable; I never felt lonely or yearned for other's attention.

I look back at my time growing up, and I can see that in many ways it was good, but it also had its bad times. I now believe all things should be done in moderation, but our life out in the bush was the extreme. However, that was the culture I was in, being only one of thousands of young people living the same life with only one difference – I was a girl; and most girls didn't have the chores or responsibilities I did, especially with the cows and as a nomad having to fend for myself. What I did, was for boys.

~

What was the most difficult thing you had to do living in the village and growing up?

Living with certain people - the teasing, the ridicule and criticism, being picked on, being in that environment. On a daily basis, herding the cows was the happiest for me, being away by myself. But the judging, not being nice, mean, criticizing, as a little kid the abuse affected me. God bless his soul, my uncle Abdi had a lot to do with my insecurity and self-doubt. He was the one that used to tell me I was too dark, had a big nose that is why my dad divorced my mother, because I was too ugly. Oh yeah and the worse of all I looked like a lizard. He would say no one would marry me. Somehow, I was dirty, disgusted, thinking something was wrong with me, I was damaged goods.

As a child it affects you mentally. No acknowledgement from others of what you go through, not being able to tell anyone, carrying a burning fire but being the only one to see it, only you no one else. When I got older, the fighting was very difficult. I put up a good fight; I may have lost, but I fought hard, not just a little. Sometimes, I'd beat guys up who were trying to attack me, I'd kick them in the crotch as that was the only way to slow them down. When I was younger, I was more vulnerable and very afraid, that's what really hurts. Not being able to go to a person's face and tell them how you feel, and not being able to defend yourself. The attacks and the fighting happened especially as a nomad.

❧

How did being in Dadaab prepare you for America?

I learned to read, even if it was a tiny amount of Somali; I learned math, even if it was just adding, subtracting, multiplying and dividing. I became a bit more modern, interacting with normal people, not just shepherds and camel boys. I learned how to ride a bus and how to shop. I learned a little about medicine and going to doctor.

I also learned how to live in a crowded environment. Before that, I spent most of my time out in the countryside by myself. In Dadaab, I was surrounded by one hundred and fifty thousand people all living in tents about fifty feet from one another. Not that America is so crowded, but I now live in a small city, and it's certainly more crowded than the grasslands of Somalia. Dadaab was, in a way, my "getting ready path" for America. I don't know that I would have survived had I came directly from the village to America

ح

Is America what you thought it would be?

For immigrants, it's a lot harder; you have to work three times harder than anyone else in school or work or anywhere else. I worked hard to be where I am today. But you set your own limitations. Any immigrant - I know what they go through; it's very hard. I know how much effort and time they have to put in if they want to be successful. I realize I'm creating a life for my kids; it's why I get up every day and go to work, do what I do, why I pay for a tutor in the summer. However, I'd be just as motivated if it were just me. I think what motivates me is that I'm the first one of all my siblings who ever finished school or college. Unfortunately, when I tell my family – no one seems to understand what I have accomplished, or how hard I had to work to get to where I am today. I typically get no response from my father when I tell him I'm done with school and work as a nurse; he just says "okay."

For some reason I'm still that little girl seeking for her dad's approval and praise. If he could only say," I'm so proud of you; look at what you have accomplished, Habibo, and I'm so sorry I was not there when you were growing up". Just those few words would mean so much more to me personally, and it would enhance my healing process. As a young girl, according to those around me, I was not good enough, ugly, too black, big nose, stupid. However, time is a leveling agent, and I can show them, "Look at me now."

∽

Do you want to write another book?

Yes, I want to call it *An Unlikely Friendship* about a middle aged Irish man who met a Somali nomad, and how they made a book together – eventually!

Bibliography

U.S. Department of State, Diplomacy in Action. September 26, 2011. Bureau of African Affairs: Somalia. http:;//www.state.gov/r/pa/ei/bgn/2863.htm

Dadaab: The World's Biggest Refugee Camp Al Jazeera, 11 July 2011. http://english.aljazeera.net/indepth/features/2011/07/201171182844876473.htm.

The Boolean 2011: Dadaab a Forgotten City in the 21st Century (Damien McSweeny)
    Somalia – History; Encyclopedia of the Nations. http://www.nationsencyclopedia.com/Africa/Somalia-HISTORY.html

International Medical Corps. ttp://internationalmedicalcorps.org.

CPSIA information can be obtained
at www.ICGtesting.com
Printed in the USA
LVOW01s2129210217
525003LV00009B/551/P